Puppet Types and Providers

Dan Bode and Nan Liu

O'REILLY®

Beijing · Cambridge · Farnham · Köln · Sebastopol · Tokyo

Puppet Types and Providers

by Dan Bode and Nan Liu

Published by O'Reilly Media, Inc., 1005 Gravenstein Highway North, Sebastopol, CA 95472.

O'Reilly books may be purchased for educational, business, or sales promotional use. Online editions are also available for most titles (*http://my.safaribooksonline.com*). For more information, contact our corporate/institutional sales department: 800-998-9938 or *corporate@oreilly.com*.

Editors: Mike Loukides and Courtney Nash	**Proofreader:** O'Reilly Production Services
Production Editor: Kristen Borg	**Cover Designer:** Karen Montgomery
	Interior Designer: David Futato
	Illustrator: Kara Ebrahim

December 2012:   First Edition

Revision History for the First Edition:

2012-12-11   First release

See *http://oreilly.com/catalog/errata.csp?isbn=9781449339326* for release details.

ISBN: 978-1-449-33932-6

[LSI]

Table of Contents

Preface

Puppet is a configuration management tool that has enjoyed phenomenal growth over the last few years. Propelled by increasing demands on sysadmins, and the continuous growth of infrastructure (both physical and virtual), Puppet has been one of the key technology components of the DevOps movement. This cultural shift focuses on breaking down the silo between development and operations. Tools like Puppet are important to this movement because it allows application deployment knowledge to be expressed as code to build automated release platforms.

Puppet is also helping lead the path towards software-defined infrastructure (or infrastructure as code). As more systems in data centers support better APIs, the importance of centralized configuration management increases. Puppet is leading this trend by leveraging its model to manage more than the roles of individual systems. It also supports network devices, load balancers, and managing virtual machine instances.

All system configurations in Puppet are expressed as resources that model complex configurations using Puppet's Domain Specific Language (DSL). Puppet supports a large set of native resources for modeling the desired state of a system. Resources already exist for managing most common elements of a system (users, groups, packages, services). These native resources are implemented in Ruby using Puppet's type and provider APIs.

The power of Puppet lies in its ability to manage the state of complex systems using this simple resource model. This book discusses the highly extensible resource model and the framework around it. It explores the extension points and how to leverage them to expand Puppet's functionality.

Puppet has a vibrant user community, and has seen an explosion of content in the last few years. Puppet's online documentation and existing books serve as great references for language constructs and architecture. We have always considered the type and provider APIs as one of the most important and least documented aspects of Puppet. This book is aimed at lowering the barrier for writing types and providers by providing sufficient instructions and examples.

Most of what we learned about types and providers has been through trial and error following the evolution of Puppet's source code changes. The experience of writing a large number of types and providers has really opened us to the potential of Puppet. Learning how to do it by reading source code, however, has been a long and painful process fraught with many mistakes and poor implementations.

The goal of this book is to explain all of the concepts of types and providers in detail along with many of the lessons we have learned. We hope this helps Puppet users better understand why they should be writing types and providers, and also arm them with enough information on how to properly implement them.

The book walks through examples to demonstrate concepts and also shows the user how to delve into Puppet's source code to get a better understanding of how types and providers are implemented internally.

It's also worth noting that when we explore the APIs for developing custom types and providers (in Chapter 2 and Chapter 3, respectively), we occasionally reimplement functionality that already exists in the Puppet source code. The examples in this book are not intended to be replacement code per se—they are intentionally simplified and intended to serve as an reference on how to implement the important features from the type and provider APIs.

Who Is This Book For?

This book is targeted at users who have a fundamental understanding of Linux/Unix systems and familiarity with basic Puppet concepts. This book is not intended to provide details of the basic language constructs of Puppet, simply enough details to discuss implementing custom Puppet resources via Ruby. It assumes that readers already have experience writing Puppet manifests and does not cover these concepts. For more information on topics specific to the Puppet DSL (classes, defines, nodes, etc.), we recommend checking out the official documentation at the Puppet Labs website (*http:// docs.puppetlabs.com*).

This book was also written to serve as a reference for developers who are writing and maintaining custom resource types. It explains the concepts required for extending Puppet by implementing custom resources as types and providers, and contains many code examples written in Ruby. It assumes that readers have some familiarity with coding, but it also explains most Ruby concepts as they are introduced.

What Does This Book Cover?

This book focuses on how Puppet is extended by creating custom resource types using the type and provider APIs. We provide an overview on Puppet resources and terminology then dive into writing types and providers in Ruby. This book is broken down into the following chapters:

- Chapter 1, **Puppet Resources** : This chapter provides an in-depth explanation of the characteristics of resources. In Puppet, resources are the basic building blocks used to model configuration state. A basic understanding of resources is required to understand what the rest of this book will be teaching about the type and provider APIs.

- Chapter 2, **Types**: This chapter covers Puppet's type API, focusing on how it is used to create new resource types that Puppet can manage, along with the list of attributes used to describe them.

- Chapter 3, **Providers**: This chapter covers the provider API, explaining how providers interact with the underlying system in order to achieve the desired state of a declared resource.

- Chapter 4, **Advanced Types and Providers**: This chapter expands the discussion of the type and provider APIs with some more advanced concepts.

Resources

- Puppet online documentation (*http://docs.puppetlabs.com*)
- Twitter, @bodepd (*http://twitter.com/bodepd*)
- Twitter, @sesshin (*http://twitter.com/sesshin*)

Conventions Used in This Book

The following typographical conventions are used in this book:

Italic
> Indicates new terms, URLs, email addresses, filenames, and file extensions.

`Constant width`
> Used for program listings, as well as within paragraphs to refer to program elements such as variable or function names, databases, data types, environment variables, statements, and keywords.

`Constant width bold`
> Shows commands or other text that should be typed literally by the user.

`Constant width italic`

> Shows text that should be replaced with user-supplied values or by values determined by context.

 This icon signifies a tip, suggestion, or general note.

 This icon indicates a warning or caution.

Using Code Examples

This book is here to help you get your job done. In general, if this book includes code examples, you may use the code in this book in your programs and documentation. You do not need to contact us for permission unless you're reproducing a significant portion of the code. For example, writing a program that uses several chunks of code from this book does not require permission. Selling or distributing a CD-ROM of examples from O'Reilly books does require permission. Answering a question by citing this book and quoting example code does not require permission. Incorporating a significant amount of example code from this book into your product's documentation does require permission.

We appreciate, but do not require, attribution. An attribution usually includes the title, author, publisher, and ISBN. For example: "*Puppet Types and Providers* by Dan Bode and Nan Liu (O'Reilly). Copyright 2013 Dan Bode and Nan Liu, 978-1-449-33932-6."

If you feel your use of code examples falls outside fair use or the permission given above, feel free to contact us at *permissions@oreilly.com*.

Safari® Books Online

 *Safari Books Online* is an on-demand digital library that delivers expert content in both book and video form from the world's leading authors in technology and business.

Technology professionals, software developers, web designers, and business and creative professionals use Safari Books Online as their primary resource for research, problem solving, learning, and certification training.

Safari Books Online offers a range of product mixes and pricing programs for organizations, government agencies, and individuals. Subscribers have access to thousands of books, training videos, and prepublication manuscripts in one fully searchable database

---

from publishers like O'Reilly Media, Prentice Hall Professional, Addison-Wesley Professional, Microsoft Press, Sams, Que, Peachpit Press, Focal Press, Cisco Press, John Wiley & Sons, Syngress, Morgan Kaufmann, IBM Redbooks, Packt, Adobe Press, FT Press, Apress, Manning, New Riders, McGraw-Hill, Jones & Bartlett, Course Technology, and dozens more. For more information about Safari Books Online, please visit us online.

How to Contact Us

Please address comments and questions concerning this book to the publisher:

O'Reilly Media, Inc.
1005 Gravenstein Highway North
Sebastopol, CA 95472
800-998-9938 (in the United States or Canada)
707-829-0515 (international or local)
707-829-0104 (fax)

We have a web page for this book, where we list errata, examples, and any additional information. You can access this page at *http://oreil.ly/puppet-types-providers*.

To comment or ask technical questions about this book, send email to *bookquestions@oreilly.com*.

For more information about our books, courses, conferences, and news, see our website at *http://www.oreilly.com*.

Find us on Facebook: *http://facebook.com/oreilly*

Follow us on Twitter: *http://twitter.com/oreillymedia*

Watch us on YouTube: *http://www.youtube.com/oreillymedia*

Acknowledgement

Thanks to Luke Kanies for writing Puppet: without all of your hard work, this book would obviously never have been written. Thanks to Teyo Tryee for providing us with guidance, but mostly for trusting and believing in us. Special thanks to both Michelle Roberts, Chris Spencer, and Joe Topjian for their support in writing this book. Michelle and Chris, thanks for making our sentences less offensive to English professors everywhere. Joe, you are the audience that we had in mind for this book; thanks for your comments on which parts of the book you felt were less clear. Thanks as well to Ken Barber and James Turnbull for your review and comments.

## CHAPTER 1

Puppet Resources

Resources are the fundamental building blocks used to model system state in Puppet. They describe the desired end state of unique elements managed by Puppet on the system. Everything that Puppet manages is expressed as a resource. In fact, every interaction between Puppet and the underlying system is expressed as a resource, too. This chapter covers the fundamental concepts behind resources, and lays out the structure of Puppet's Resource Model for types and providers, setting you up to dive into both in the later chapters.

Installing Puppet
Given that this book is aimed at existing Puppet users, we assume you already have it installed. However, if you don't, check out Appendix A, and then jump back here to get started.

Resources describe the desired end state of system components by specifying a type, a title, and a list of attributes.

Type
The type of a resource determines the system component Puppet manages. Some common types are: user, group, file, service and package. A resource declaration always contains the type of resource being managed.

Title
The title of a resource identifies an instance of that resource type. The combination of type and title refers to a single unique element managed by puppet, such as a user name *joe* or a file with path */root/.bashrc*.

Attributes

Each resource supports a list of key value pairs called attributes. These attributes provide a detailed description that Puppet uses to manage the resource. For example, the file */root/.bashrc* should be present. The user *dan* should be present and have its login shell set to */bin/bash*.

Puppet provides a Domain Specific Language (DSL) that expresses the intended state of a system's configuration through collections of resources. Resources are declared in Puppet's DSL with the following syntax:

```
<type> { <title> :
  attribute1 => value1,
  attribute2 => value2,
}
```

The following specific example is applied by Puppet to ensure that a package named *apache2* is installed:

```
package { 'apache2':
  ensure => present,
}
```

You can combine several resources together to create a manifest (a source file for Puppet code) using the Puppet DSL. Manifests often contain classes that are used to create collections of resources which provide a common application or service.

The following manifest ensures that the latest version of the *apache2* package is installed, and checks that the service is running on the web servers managed by Puppet:

```
class webserver {

  package { 'apache2':
    ensure => latest,
  }

  service { 'apache2':
    ensure    => running,
    subscribe => Package['apache2'],
  }

}
```

This description can be applied to any node to ensure it is configured as a web server. The following example demonstrates how the the node *web1* is designated as a web server:

```
node 'web1' {
  class { 'webserver': }
}
```

Figure 1-1 shows how the webserver class is applied to several machines.

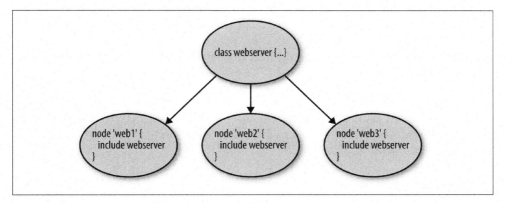

Figure 1-1. Configuring multiple nodes as webservers

Resource Characteristics

Understanding how resources behave is extremely important for the following chapters on types and providers. A clear understanding of Puppet resources allows you to effectively develop custom resources using Puppet's type and provider APIs that are consistent with Puppet's model. Both the type and provider APIs are used to implement resources that will be declared in Puppet's DSL. This section will cover a few fundamental characteristics of resources, including:

- Declarative
- Idempotent
- Unique

Declarative

Resources describe what Puppet should manage without having to specify any information related to the procedure or process that should be used. This is the defining characteristic of being *declarative*. This is in contrast to scripting languages where the author must specify a sequence of actions to configure the system. To manage a system with Puppet you only have to describe the desired state of each resource.

The example resource below declares an `ftp` service account:

```
user { 'ftp':
  ensure => present,
  shell  => '/sbin/nologin',
}
```

When applied to a system, Puppet ensures that this user:

- Exists on the system
- Has its shell set to /sbin/nologin (meaning that the system will not allow remote logins for that user)

This resource can be declared without having to specify (or even know) the exact procedure required to ensure that the end result is a system user with those characteristics. The details of how this user is managed are handled by Puppet and abstracted away from the person writing the manifest.

Idempotent

Idempotent is a math term that applies to operations always resulting in the same outcome regardless of how many times they are applied. In the world of Puppet, this simply means that a resource can be applied to a system multiple times and the end result will always be the same.

Consider the resource from our previous example:

```
user { 'ftp':
  ensure => present,
  shell  => '/sbin/nologin',
}
```

Since resources are declarative, the end state of the `ftp` account should always be the same regardless of the starting state of the system. If the system is already in the desired state, then Puppet will not perform any action. This means that resources can be applied any number of times and the result will always be the same.

Consider the states that could exist on a system before we apply our example resource to it:

- The user does not exist
- The user exists and has its shell set to *sbin/nologin*
- The user exists but its shell is not set to *sbin/nologin*

As shown in Figure 1-2, the end state of our system is always the same because resources in Puppet are declarative and idempotent. Users can declare the resulting state that will exist after Puppet has been applied, without having to care about or even know the current state of the system.

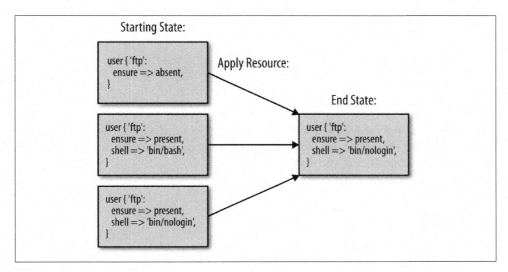

Figure 1-2. Puppet resource state

With procedural scripts, the author must specify how to modify a resource into the desired end state for each of the starting cases specified above. This is why procedural scripts are rarely idempotent—there is too much logic required to handle every possible starting case correctly.

To achieve the same behavior as Puppet, users need to write complex logic to ensure that each command is only executed conditionally when changes need to be made to the underlying system. The following shell script reimplements our example ftp user resource:

```
#!/bin/bash
set -e
set -u
if getent passwd ftp; then
  USER_LOGIN=`getent passwd ftp | cut -d: -f7`
  if [ '/sbin/nologin' != "${USER_LOGIN}" ]; then
    usermod -s /sbin/nologin ftp
  fi
else
  useradd -s /sbin/nologin ftp
fi
```

The shell script detects if the user already exists, as well as the user's current shell, in order to decide if any changes need to be made. Puppet's user resource supports many more properties than just *shell*. Just imagine how complex the bash equivalent to the following resource would be!

```
user { 'ftp':
  ensure => present,
```

```
    shell  => '/sbin/nologin',
    home   => '/var/lib/ftp',
    uid    => '601',
    gid    => 'system',
}
```

Unique

Resources in Puppet must be *unique*. Because each resource declares a desired end state, duplicates of the same resource (identified by a unique combination of type and title) could result in a conflicting end state.

The following resources declare two conflicting `ftp` users:

```
user { 'ftp':
  ensure => present,
  uid    => 501,
}

user { 'ftp':
  ensure => present,
  uid    => 502,
}
```

This manifest specifies that the `ftp` user's `uid` should be both 501 and 502.

Fortunately, Puppet enforces unique combinations of type and title across all resources. If Puppet detects duplicate resources when processing a manifest, it prevents conflicts by failing with the error below:

```
Duplicate declaration: User[ftp] is already declared in file user.pp at line 4;
cannot redeclare at user.pp:9 on node my_host
```

Puppet's ability to detect duplicate resource declarations is extremely handy when combining collections of resources from different modules. Any conflicting state between collections of resources results in a failure and a clear error message. This prevents users from deploying applications with conflicting requirements.

Resource Model

Puppet's Resource Model consists of two layers called *types* and *providers*. Types specify the interfaces used to describe resources in Puppet's DSL and providers encapsulate the procedure used to manage those resources on a specific platform. A resource uses the interface defined by its type to declare a list of attributes that describe its state. The provider uses these declared attributes to manage the state of a resource.

As an example, a user account may contains settings like username, group, and home directory. These attributes are defined as a part of its type. These users are managed differently on Windows, Linux, or ldap. The methods to create, destroy, and modify accounts are implemented as a separate provider for each of these backends.

We'll dive into types and providers in much more detail in the following chapters—in the rest of this chapter, we'll set the stage with some basic concepts for both.

Types

The Type API expresses the interface used to declaratively describe a resource. In Puppet, there are two kinds of types: *defined* types written in Puppet's DSL, and *native* types that are written in Ruby. Puppet ships with a large collection of native resources implemented in Ruby. This includes basic things like: *users*, *groups*, *packages*, *services*, and *files* (and some not-so-basic things like *zfs/zones*).

Defined types create an interface around a composition of resources. Consider the following defined type:

```
define custom_user (
    $ensure = present,
    $home
) {
    # …. omitting resources composing custom_user.
}
```

As we saw earlier, a resource (in this case, custom_user) is defined by providing a resource title and the attributes $ensure and $home. This defined type can be consumed without worrying about the resources that provide the implementation:

```
custom_user { 'ftp':
    ensure => present,
    home   => '/var/lib/ftp',
}
```

Ruby Types provide the ability to specify resource interfaces just like the define keyword in the Puppet DSL. They are implemented using the type API, which offers a much richer descriptive language and provides additional features such as validation and resource dependencies (we'll look at this in much greater depth in the next chapter).

Ruby types, unlike defined types, rely on providers for the procedures used to manage the underlying system.

Providers

Providers implement the procedure used to manage resources. A resource is simply declared as a list of attributes because all of the instructions for managing that resource have been encapsulated in the provider. Additionally, multiple providers can be implemented for a single type, allowing the same resource to be applied on different operating systems.

Puppet includes one or more providers for each of its native types. For example, Puppet's User type includes eight different providers that implement support across a variety of Unix, Linux, and even Windows platforms.

The Package type (as shown below) contains the most providers:

```
$ ls ~/src/puppet/lib/puppet/provider/package/
aix.rb      blastwave.rb  macports.rb     pkg.rb      rpm.rb          yum.rb
appdmg.rb  dpkg.rb        msi.rb          pkgdmg.rb   rug.rb          yumhelper.py
apple.rb   fink.rb        nim.rb          pkgutil.rb  sun.rb          zypper.rb
apt.rb     freebsd.rb     openbsd.rb      portage.rb  sunfreeware.rb
aptitude.rb gem.rb        pacman.rb       ports.rb    up2date.rb
aptrpm.rb  hpux.rb pip.r  portupgrade.rb  urpmi.rb
```

 These examples assume you installed Puppet from source in *~/src/* as outlined in Appendix A. Future references to source code also make this assumption.

Providers are one of the most common sources of community contributions to Puppet Core. One of the most powerful things about Puppet is the amount of operational systems knowledge already encoded into its native providers.

To find all of the providers that are currently part of Puppet, have a look in the provider directory of the Puppet source code:

```
$ find ~/src/puppet/lib/puppet/provider/ -type f
```

In order to contribute a provider to an existing type, a developer only has to implement two basic pieces of functionality:

1. How to query the current state of this resource
2. How to configure the system to reflect the desired state

Implementing this functionality will be explained in detail in Chapter 3.

The puppet resource Command

The `puppet resource` command-line tool allows users to interact with resources by querying and modifying the underlying system. This tool provides the ability to interact with resources using the same API that is used when they are managed by the Puppet DSL.

This provides a great way for beginners to become more familiar with how resources function by seeing how they interact with the underlying system. It is also a great debugging tool for developing providers.

Retrieving Resources

The `puppet resource` command interacts directly with resources implemented in Ruby. It relies on the provider to retrieve a list of resource instances on the system where the command is executed. The command also accepts the type and title that uniquely identify the resource to be queried:

```
# puppet resource <type> <title>
```

The following example shows that the `ftp` user does not currently exist on the system:

```
# puppet resource user ftp
user { 'ftp':
  ensure => 'absent',
}
```

The current state of this resource is returned to STDOUT in a format compatible with Puppet's DSL. In fact, the output could be redirected from this command to create a valid Puppet manifest which could then be applied:

```
puppet resource user ftp > ftp_user.pp
puppet apply ftp_user.pp
```

Modifying Resources

`puppet resource` can also modify the current state of resources on the underlying system. It accepts resource attributes as key value pairs from the command line using the following syntax:

```
$ puppet resource <type> <title> ensure=<resource_state>  <attribute1>=<value1>
<attribute2>=<value2> ...
```

The following example declares that our ftp user should exist with its home directory set as */var/lib/ftp*. If the system did not have an ftp user when this command was executed, you should see the following output:

```
$ puppet resource user ftp ensure=present home='/var/lib/ftp'
notice: /User[ftp]/ensure: created
```

```
user { 'ftp':
  ensure => 'present',
  home   => '/var/lib/ftp',
}
```

The message above indicates that Puppet has created this user. Once the account exists on the system, subsequent Puppet runs will simply complete without notice messages indicating there were no changes to the system. This also demonstrates the idempotent nature of Puppet that we discussed earlier:

```
$ puppet resource user ftp ensure=present home='/var/lib/ftp'
user { 'ftp':
  ensure => 'present',
  home   => '/var/lib/ftp',
}
```

If the user exists, we can use puppet resource to query for the current state of that account:

```
$ puppet resource user ftp
user { 'ftp':
  ensure           => 'present',
  gid              => '1004',
  home             => '/var/lib/ftp',
  password         => '!',
  password_max_age => '99999',
  password_min_age => '0',
  shell            => '/bin/bash',
  uid              => '1003',
}
```

 puppet resource returns more attributes than those that we explicitly specified for that user. It actually returns all properties for the resource being queried. Properties will be explained in detail in Chapter 2.

The puppet resource command also updates individual attributes of a resource that already exists:

```
$ puppet resource user ftp shell=/sbin/nologin --debug
debug: User[ftp](provider=useradd):  ↪
  Executing '/usr/sbin/usermod -s /sbin/nologin ftp'
notice: /User[ftp]/shell: shell changed '/bin/bash' to '/sbin/nologin'
...
user { 'ftp':
  ensure => 'present',
  shell  => '/sbin/nologin',
}
```

Running `puppet resource` with the debug option (`--debug`) allows you to see the system commands executed by that resource's provider.

The results above contain two lines of output worth mentioning:

```
debug: User[ftp](provider=useradd): ↪
    Executing '/usr/sbin/usermod -s /sbin/nologin ftp'
```

The `debug` output shows that the `useradd` provider modifies the current shell with the `usermod` command. This information serves as a useful debugging tool. Users can troubleshoot failures using the exact same commands Puppet does, directly from their shell.

```
notice: /User[ftp]/shell: shell changed '/bin/bash' to '/sbin/nologin'
```

The above message, logged at notice level, shows how the modification to the underlying system is treated as a state transition (the state of the ftp user's `shell` attribute has transitioned from */bin/bash* to */sbin/nologin*). Puppet treats all updates to the system as state transitions and records them as events.

Run the same command again and note that no events occur when the system state already matches the desired state:

```
# puppet resource --debug user ftp shell=/sbin/nologin
```

This reiterates the idempotent nature of resources: Puppet does not perform any changes if the system already matches the desired state.

Discover All Resources

We have already shown how Puppet can retrieve the current state of individual resources. It can also query for all instances of a given resource type on a system. When combined, these two features allow Puppet to discover the current state of all resources of a certain type on the underlying system.

You can query for all instances of a given type using the following syntax:

```
$ puppet resource <type>
```

The following example queries all existing package resources on an Ubuntu system:

```
# puppet resource package
package { 'accountsservice':
  ensure => '0.6.15-2ubuntu9',
}
package { 'adduser':
  ensure => '3.113ubuntu2',
}
package { 'apache2':
  ensure => '2.2.22-1ubuntu1',
```

```
}
package { 'apache2-mpm-worker':
  ensure => '2.2.22-1ubuntu1',
}
...
```

This capability is implemented using the `self.instances` method, which will be explained in Chapter 3.

Noop Mode

Noop (pronounced "no-ahp") mode is a way for Puppet to simulate manifests and report pending changes. When noop mode is enabled (using the `--noop` flag), Puppet queries each resource and reports differences between the system and its desired state. This provides a safe way to understand the potential impact of applying Puppet manifests. It is common to use noop mode when running Puppet outside a change window, or when you want to get a better understanding of what kinds of changes Puppet needs to make.

The Puppet Resource Model provides this capability by breaking up resource evaluation into the following distinct phases (as shown in Figure 1-3):

1. Users declare the desired state of resources.
2. The provider discovers the current state of managed resources.
3. Puppet compares each resource's current state against the desired state.
4. If they are not the same, the provider updates the underlying system.
5. Changes to the underlying system are recorded as events.

When Puppet is run in noop mode, it skips step #4 in the list above, and records differences between desired and observed state as events without making any modifications to the system.

Catalogs

A Puppet catalog is a collection of resources compiled from a set of manifests. We've already seen the manner in which resources describe how individual components of the system should be configured. The catalog is a composition of resources that are used to model a service or a system. The catalog can be stored centrally by PuppetDB, which maintains a wealth of information about how your infrastructure is configured. The catalog is easily introspected to better understand how a system should be configured, and what dependencies might exist.

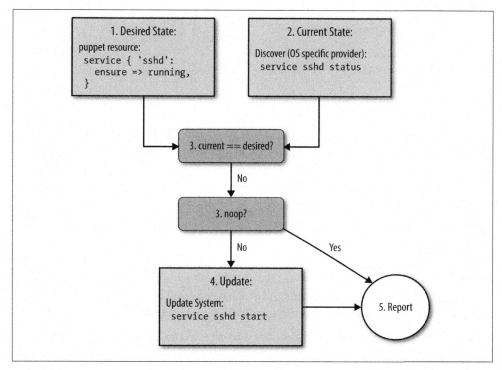

Figure 1-3. Resource evaluation phases in Puppet

Dependencies

Resources deploying an application often require individual components to be configured in a specific order. These dependencies are expressed as relationships in Puppet. The order of resources can be specified using the `require` and `before` resource metaparameters (special attributes that are accepted by every resource type) or with the `autorequire` method, which will be discussed in the next chapter. When Puppet applies a catalog, its resources will not be applied until all of their dependencies are satisfied.

These example manifests show how the `require` and `before` metaparameters can construct the same catalog:

```
package { 'apache2':
  ensure => present,
}
service { 'apache2':
  ensure  => running,
  require => Package['apache2']
}
```

```
package { 'apache2':
  ensure => present,
  before => Service['apache2'],
}
service { 'apache2':
  ensure => running,
}
```

Catalog as a Graph

The data structure of the catalog is a *graph*. Graphs are characterized as a collection of objects where some of the object pairs are interconnected. The objects are referred to as *vertices* and the the links between pairs of those objects are *edges*. As shown in Figure 1-4, the vertices of the catalog are Puppet resources, and the edges are the dependencies between those resources.

The graph that represents Puppet's catalog has two primary characteristics: it is *directed* and *acyclical*.

Directed

The Puppet Catalog is said to be a directed graph because all of its edges have a direction; that is, every edge designates the order in which a pair of resources needs to be applied.

Figure 1-5 shows how `before` and `require` add directed edges to create a graph:

```
package { 'apache2':
  ensure => present,
  before  => File['apache2'],
}
file { 'apache2':
  name     => '/etc/apache2/apache2.conf',
  content => template('apache/apache.erb'),
}
service { 'apache2':
  ensure  => running,
  require => File['apache2'],
}
```

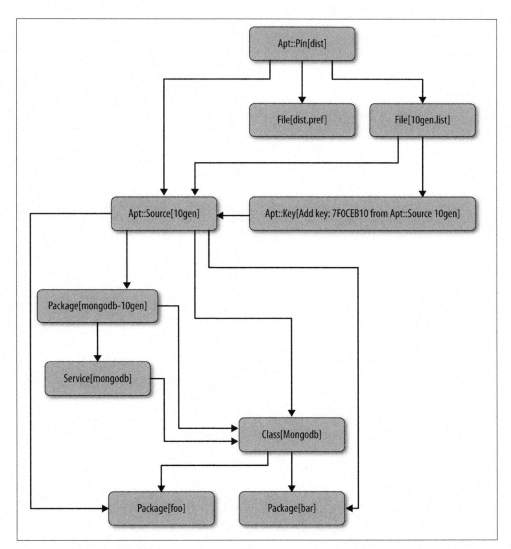

Figure 1-4. Puppet catalog graph

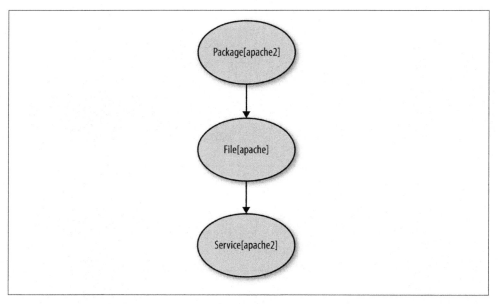

Figure 1-5. Directed edges created by **before** *and* **require**

Acyclical

Since the order in which resources are applied is indicated by the edges of the graph, it follows that there cannot be *cycles* in the graph. If cycles exist in a graph, Puppet cannot determine the order in which things should be applied.

Consider the following manifest that introduces a dependency cycle. Each resource specifies a dependency on the other resource. It Puppet interpreted these dependencies literally, it would indicate that no resources could ever be applied. Fortunately Puppet detects these kinds of cycles and fails before trying to apply the catalog.

```
package { 'apache2':
  ensure  => present,
  require => Service['apache2']
}
service { 'apache2':
  ensure  => running,
  require => Package['apache2']
}
```

Conclusion

Thus far, we've looked at the core characteristics of resources (uniqueness, idempotent, declarative), how they are composed by Puppet's DSL, and how they interact with the underlying system. With this fundamental understanding of resources, we are ready to move on to how they are created using Puppet's type and provider APIs.

## CHAPTER 2

Types

The type API expresses resources that can be leveraged from Puppet's DSL to manage the underlying system. In fact, all native resource types that ship as a part of Puppet (*packages*, *users*, *files*, *services*, …) are implemented using the type API covered in this chapter. In addition, the type API specifies the attributes for describing each resource. For example:

- Files have modes.
- Users have shells.
- Hosts have IP addresses.

This API offers developers a simple collection of Ruby methods to create resource interfaces that serve as an abstraction layer on which multiple providers can be implemented. It also allows sysadmins to describe system configuration as resources without understanding the procedures developers have implemented via providers.

This section will focus on how custom types are written in Ruby, and will cover the following:

- How to create a custom type
- How to add attributes to a type
- Special attributes
  - Namevars
  - Properties
  - ensure property
  - Parameters

- Input validation and data transformation
- Implicit resource dependencies

Defining Puppet Types

Resource types are defined by calling the `newtype` method on the `Puppet::Type` class and passing it a symbol representing the name of the type to create.

Ruby Symbols

In Ruby, symbols are constructed by placing a colon before a string (i.e., `:hello` or `:"hello"`). Symbols are often used instead of strings in Ruby for performance reasons because symbols, unlike strings, refer to a unique object. Because of this, symbols consume less memory and facilitate faster comparisons than strings.

The following example creates a custom_user resource with the `newtype` method:

```
Puppet::Type.newtype(:custom_user) do
end
```

In Ruby, the names of source files must match the namespace of the Ruby class that they contain. Since Puppet Types and Providers are implemented in Ruby, they follow this convention. Since the example above creates the Ruby class `Puppet::Type::Custom_user`, it should be located in the source file: *puppet/type/custom_user.rb*. This file should be created inside of a module like any other Puppet extension.

The directory structure below shows a module called `example` that contains the source code for our custom type.

```
`-- /etc/puppet/modules/example
    |-- lib
    |   `-- puppet
    |       |-- type
    |       |   `-- custom_user.rb
    |       `-- provider
    |               `-- ….
```

A list of all the native types that ship as part of Puppet can be retrieved by listing the contents of the *puppet/type* directory (assuming Puppet is installed from source as described in Appendix A):

```
$ ls ~/src/puppet/lib/puppet/type
```

The name of files in this directory correspond to the names of all of the native types that are distributed with Puppet. For example, Puppet's User resource is defined in the source file:

~/src/puppet/lib/puppet/type/user.rb

```
Puppet::Type.newtype(:user) do
  # lots of code...
end
```

Type Examples From Puppet Source

Some of the native types from Puppet's source code define the type by calling `newtype` on the Puppet module. Creating types using `Puppet::Type.newtype` is the recommended way going forward. Keep in mind that the existing native types may be slightly different than how the API is presented in this book. This is because the native types have evolved with Puppet. Some of the practices taught in this book may have not been available when some of the earlier types were written.

Continuing our example, let's create a custom type to manage packages called `custom_package`.

The `custom_package` type is not intended to serve as a replacement of Puppet's existing package type. It serves as an example of how to take advantage of the features of the type and provider APIs.

First, create the `custom_package` type source file in our example module:

/etc/puppet/modules/example/lib/puppet/type/custom_package.rb

```
Puppet::Type.newtype(:custom_package) do

end
```

The type code cannot be loaded by Puppet if the file source path does not match the name of the type.

Although we have created a new resource type, it cannot be declared using the Puppet DSL. A valid resource declaration requires the type, as well as a title that uniquely identifies the resource being specified. At this point, we have created a new kind of resource, namely *custom_package*, but we have not expressed any of the attributes used to manage it. As soon as we add a special attribute, called its `namevar`, we can declare our new resource in the Puppet DSL. Attributes and the `namevar` will be covered in the next section.

Attributes

The type API provides methods for creating the attributes used to describe the characteristics of a resource. When a resource is declared in the Puppet DSL, its attributes are all expressed as key value pairs:

```
type { 'title':
  key1 => 'value1',
  key2 => 'value2',
}
```

This section will walk through an example that adds the following attributes to our `custom_package` type: `name`, `ensure`, `version`, `source`, and `replace_config`. When this type is completed, it will support the description below:

```
custom_package { 'apache':
  ensure         => present,
  name           => 'apache2',
  version        => '2.2.22-1ubuntu1',
  source         => 'http://myrepo/apache2.deb',
  replace_config => yes,
}
```

Namevars

A `namevar` is a special kind of attribute that serves as the identity of a resource on the underlying system. When creating a new resource type, the first task is to choose a `namevar`. The most important property about a `namevar` is that it must uniquely identify the resource. In this sense, the `namevar` can be thought of as the resource's primary key. Most resources that need to be managed have unique identifiers:

- Path of a file
- Name of a user, group, package, or service

The name of a file, unlike many of the other native types in Puppet, is not a suitable `namevar` because it is not unique across a system. Multiple files with the same name can exist in different directories. The fully qualified file path is better suited for this purpose since each path identifies a single unique resource.

Pro Tip

Namevars should use a characteristic that can be predicted before a resource exists. For example, each Windows user is associated with a globally unique identifier (GUID) that is generated randomly when the user is created. Even though each GUID is associated with a unique user, it is not suitable as a `namevar` because the manifest's author cannot pre-specify the value when declaring a resource.

GUID is an implementation of a more general concept called a Universal Unique ID (UUID). Often, resources with UUIDs do not have another unique property that can be predetermined. In these cases, it is often necessary to pick a different characteristic as the `namevar` and have Puppet enforce the uniqueness of that attribute on the underlying system. An example is Amazon's EC2, where all machine instances are uniquely referred to by UUIDs that cannot be predicted. In this case, instance metadata can be used as a label to identify the system as long as Puppet enforces it as a unique key across all virtual machine instances in EC2.

We can set a `namevar` for our custom_package example by adding the following code:

```
Puppet::Type.newtype(:custom_package) do
  ...
  newparam(:name, :namevar => true) do
  end
end
```

In the Puppet source code, many parameters are designated as name vars with the `isnamevar` method:

```
newparam(:name) do
  isnamevar
end
```

Although `isnamevar` also serves the same purpose, using `:namevar` ⇒ `true` is the recommended style going forward for setting `namevars`. In this book, if there is more than one way to do something, we will focus on the preferred method.

Now that we have specified a `namevar` for our type, we can declare a valid resource using the `custom_package` type:

```
custom_package { 'apache': }
```

When a user omits the resource's `namevar`, Puppet defaults the value to the resource's title. Since the `custom_package` resource above is declared without the `name` attribute, the `namevar` is set to the value of its title: `apache`. Although the title and `namevar` are commonly the same, they serve two different purposes in Puppet. The title is used to reference the resource in the Puppet catalog, and the `namevar` indicates the system's name for the resource.

The example below demonstrates a situation where the `namevar` is not the same as a resource's title. The title of that resource is `apache` and its `namevar` is `httpd`. This resource can be referenced as `apache`, but the package under management is `httpd`:

```
custom_package { 'apache':
  name => 'httpd',
}
$ puppet apply -e "custom_package { 'apache': }"
notice: Finished catalog run in 0.04 seconds
```

The command above verifies that Puppet can properly load our new type and that it has a `namevar`. However, our resource declaration above does not describe anything that can be managed. The next section discusses special attributes, called properties, that specify the things that Puppet manages.

Properties

Properties are attributes that model the state of a resource on the underlying system; Puppet actively enforces their value on the system. Every time Puppet runs, it retrieves the current value of every property and compares it to the value specified in the resource declaration.

Properties are also the main integration point between types and providers. Types specify which properties exist, and providers supply the implementation details for how those properties are managed on the system.

Figuring out if an attribute should be a property is one of the most important design decisions for a resource type. In general, you can decide if an attribute should be a property by asking the following questions:

- Can I discover the state of this attribute?
- Can I update the state of this attribute?

If the answer to both of those questions is yes, then that attribute should be implemented as a property. In general, if the answer to one or both of these questions is no, then the characteristic should not be a property.

Pro Tip

Certain attributes, such as UUIDs, can be queried from the system but cannot be updated. These attributes can be implemented as read-only properties so that puppet resource still returns their value when inspecting the system.

Properties are added to types by calling Puppet::Type's newproperty method and passing it a symbol that represents the name of the property.

Our custom_package type needs a version property to manage the current version of an installed package:

```
Puppet::Type.newtype(:custom_package) do
  ...
  newproperty(:version) do
  end
end
```

Now this resource can be declared in Puppet as follows:

```
custom_package { 'apache':
  version => '2.2.22-1ubuntu1',
}
```

Applying the above resource results in failure because we have not implemented the provider methods for managing package versions. We will walk through the process of implementing these methods in the next chapter.

```
$ puppet apply -e 'custom_package { "apache": version=>1.2}'
err: /Stage[main]//Custom_package[apache]: Could not evaluate: undefined method
`version' for nil:NilClass
notice: Finished catalog run in 0.04 seconds
```

Now that you understand what properties are, let's discuss a special property called ensure.

The ensure Property

ensure is a property that models the existence of a resource. Most resource types support the ensurable property, meaning that their existence on the system can be discovered and managed by Puppet. Some examples of native types that are not ensurable are Exec, Notify, and Stage.

You add the ensure property to a type with the ensurable method:

```
Puppet::Type.newtype(:custom_package) do
  ensurable
  ...
end
```

This method adds the `ensure` property to our resource type, which accepts two values. Providers manage the `ensure` property by implementing the `create`, `exists?`, and `destroy` methods. The implementation of these methods will be explained in detail in the next chapter.

We can now use the `ensure` property to describe that a resource should exist:

```
custom_package { 'apache':
  ensure => present,
}
```

Or that it should not exist:

```
custom_package { 'apache':
  ensure => absent,
}
```

Properties are only used to express things that need to be managed by Puppet. The next section discusses another type of attribute, called parameters.

Parameters

Parameters supply additional information to providers, which is used to manage its properties. In contrast with properties, parameters are not discovered from the system and cannot be created or updated.

Parameters allow you to specify additional context or the ability to override a provider's default behavior. For example, the service resource supports the following parameters: start, stop, status, and restart. None of these attributes reflect the state of a service. Instead, they *override* the commands a provider uses to interact with services on the system.

You may have now realized that the `namevar`, which we discussed earlier, is also a parameter. Changing the `namevar` of a resource does not cause a resource instance's state to be modified, it indicates that a different resource is being managed.

Our `custom_package` example needs a parameter called `source` to instruct the provider where it can find the package to install. The following code adds this parameter:

```
Puppet::Type.newtype(:custom_package) do
  ...
  newparam(:source) do
  end
end
```

Now you can provide the location of a package to install:

```
custom_package { 'apache':
  ensure => present,
  source => 'http://package_repo/apache.rpm',
}
```

Puppet can't determine the source that was used to install an existing package. It also can't update the source used to install a package. The source is only used by the provider during installation to update the ensure property.

Some packages include default configuration files. Package providers typically support the ability to indicate during upgrades whether new packages should override existing configuration files. By default, customized configuration files are retained during software upgrades.

The code below adds an additional parameter to determine whether or not our `cus tom_package` resources should override existing configuration files during upgrade operations:

```
Puppet::Type.newtype(:custom_package) do
  ...
  newparam(:replace_config) do
  end
end
```

As mentioned before, packages typically do not replace existing configuration files by default. In the next section, we'll discuss how a default value can be specified for the replace_config parameter.

Default Values

The `defaultto` method is used to specify default values for any attribute. Defaults are typically only specified for parameters. They are less common for properties because a default value will result in that property *always* being managed (there is no way to unset a value for the property).

The `replace_config` parameter from our example should default to "no" (indicating that upgrade operations should not override existing configuration files). Default values are specified for any parameter or property with `defaultto`:

```
Puppet::Type.newtype(:custom_package) do
  newparam(:replace_config) do
    defaultto :no
  end
end
```

Defaults should not be specified for an attribute unless it is universally applicable to all instances of that resource. Puppet provides a convenient syntax to specify resource defaults in the DSL which is generally preferred for properties:

```
Custom_package {
  ensure => present,
}
custom_package { ['package_one', 'package_two']: }
```

The next section will discuss type API methods that support validating resource declarations.

Input Validation

Input validation supplied by the type API provides informative error messages when resources are declared with invalid attribute values. Input validation occurs before any resources are applied, so a failure will prevent the entire catalog from being applied.

There are two methods that support validation in the Type API: `validate` and `newvalues`.

Validate

The `validate` method validates parameters, properties, and the complete state of the resources being declared. When an attribute value is declared, Puppet will invoke the validate method if defined. This method will always be called if a default value is supplied. Validate can also be called on the type itself—this allows you to enforce required attributes or validate combinations of attribute values.

Validate accepts a block where the validation rules are implemented:

```
validate do |value|
  # block of code
end
```

Ruby Blocks

The syntax do/end in Ruby indicates that a block of code is being passed as an argument to a method.

If the resource is invalid, the validation block should raise an exception and Puppet will not apply the catalog. The `fail` method can be used to raise a `Puppet::Error` exception accompanied by a sensible message explaining why the validation error has occurred.

Ruby Exceptions

Exceptions are used in Ruby to indicate an error has occurred that affects the normal operation of a program. Exceptions in Puppet are usually of the `Puppet::Error` class.

In our `custom_package` example, we should verify that users supplied a valid source path or URL, as well as a sensible version string.

First, let's use Ruby's built-in libraries Pathname and URI to express that valid sources are either absolute filepaths or HTTP URIs:

```
require 'pathname'
require 'uri'
Puppet::Type.newtype(:custom_package) do
  newparam(:source) do
    validate do |value|
      unless Pathname.new(value).absolute? ||
              URI.parse(value).is_a?(URI::HTTP)
        fail("Invalid source #{value}")
      end
    end
  end
end
```

The following example shows how to specify the valid character sets that can be used to compose our package versions:

```
Puppet::Type.newtype(:custom_package) do
  ...
  newproperty(:version) do
    validate do |value|
      fail("Invalid version #{value}") unless value =~ /^[0-9A-Za-z\.-]+$/
    end
  end
end
```

 Ruby Regular Expressions
Regular expressions in Ruby are denoted with a leading and trailing forward slash (i.e., /\d+/).

The next example uses global validation to specify that a source must always be set when ensure is present. Any resource attribute's value can be accessed via self with the attribute symbol as the key:

```
Puppet::Type.newtype(:custom_package) do
  ...
  validate do
      fail('source is required when ensure is present') if self[:ensure]
== :present and self[:source].nil?
  end
end
```

newvalues

The newvalues method restricts attributes to a list of valid values. This list is composed of an array of strings, symbols or regular expressions. This provides a much more concise method than the validate method for restricting an attribute to a set of valid values.

 The newvalues and newvalue methods are not the same. newvalues only expresses valid values, while newvalue expresses how specific values trigger certain provider methods. newvalues is valid for all attributes while newvalue is only valid for properties.

The example code below demonstrates how to restrict the values for the replace_config parameter to only accept yes or no:

```
Puppet::Type.newtype(:custom_package) do
  newparam(:replace_config) do
    defaultto :no
    newvalues(:yes, :no)
  end
end
```

The newvalues method also accepts regular expressions as an argument. The following example restricts values of source to either absolute paths or http(s):

```
Puppet::Type.newtype(:custom_package) do
  ...
  newparam(:source) do
    newvalues(/https?:\/\//, /\//)
  end
end
```

After Puppet performs validation for its types, it is possible to transform the attribute's inputs to a specific format. The next section will discuss how this is implemented using the munge method.

munge

The munge method is used to transform user input before Puppet compares it to the values returned by the provider. To determine if a property needs to be updated, Puppet performs a simple equality comparison between the current value and the value retrieved by the provider. munge can ensure the user-supplied data type is consistent with the values returned by the provider.

For the following custom_user resource, munge ensures that the retrieved value is always compared against an integer. This enables the users to specify either a number or a numeric string value for uid:

```
Puppet::Type.newtype(:custom_user) do
  newparam(:uid) do
    munge do |value|
      Integer(value)
    end
  end
end
```

 When both munging and validation are specified for an attribute, the validation method always occurs before munging.

AutoRequire

The `autorequire` method builds implicit ordering between resources in the catalog. This allows types to specify well established dependencies that should always exist between certain resources. Many Puppet types take advantage of this feature to prevent users from having to explicitly declare tedious relationships between resources:

- Files always depend on their parent directories.
- Users always depend on their groups

For example, if the `custom_package` source parameter is a local filepath, then we always want to ensure this file is managed before the package is installed:

```
Puppet::Type.newtype(:custom_package) do
  ...
  autorequire(:file) do
    self[:source] if self[:source] and Pathname.new(self[:source]).absolute?
  end
end
```

Unlike resource dependencies specified in the Puppet DSL, this is a soft dependency— it is only specified if the required resources it depends on exist in the catalog. The manifest below does not include the file resource *tmp/apache.deb*. However it can be applied without errors:

```
custom_package { 'apache':
  ensure => present,
  source => '/tmp/apache.deb',
}
```

Dependencies in the Puppet DSL have a higher precedence than any implicit dependencies specified with the `autorequire` method. This can be handy for cases such as uninstallation, where the order in which resources need to be applied is reversed. The example below does not create a dependency cycle, because the `require` parameter set in the file resource will override the implicit dependency.

```
custom_package { 'apache':
  ensure => absent,
  source => '/tmp/apache.deb',
}
file { '/tmp/apache.deb':
  ensure => absent,
  require => Custom_package['apache'],
}
```

All of the examples that we have seen so far used simple primitives to assign a single value to each attribute—Puppet is able to handle strings, integers, and booleans this way. The next section will explain how arrays are used as attribute inputs.

Arrays

Arrays are used to assign a list of values to an attribute. If a resource of type `cus tom_user` called *foo* belongs to multiple groups, then this attribute would be supplied as an array:

```
custom_user { 'foo':
  ensure => present,
  groups => ['admin', 'developer'],
}
```

When the expected value of an attribute is an array, there are a couple of additional things that need to be implemented in the type.

You need to pass in the option `array_matching` with its value set to `all`. This tells Puppet to treat all values of the array as the value for that attribute:

```
Puppet::Type.newtype(:custom_user) do
  newproperty(:groups, :array_matching => :all) do
  end
end
```

Inline Documentation

Once you've finished writing your custom type, you'll want to provide some documentation about it. Inline documentation can be embedded in the Ruby source code using the `desc` method, which can be called on the type itself as well as for each parameter and property of that type.

Then users can retrieve your inline documentation with either the `puppet describe` or `puppet doc` command.

For full documentation of all types currently configured in your puppet environment, including custom resources installed via Puppet modules, run the following command:

```
$ puppet describe --list
```

Let's complete our example custom_package type with full inline documentation:

```
Puppet::Type.newtype(:custom_package) do

  desc 'custom_package is an example of how to write a Puppet type.'

  ensurable

  newparam(:name, :namevar => true) do
    desc 'The name of the software package.'
  end

  newproperty(:version) do
    desc 'version of a package that should be installed'
    validate do |value|
      fail("Invalid version #{value}") unless value =~ /^[0-9A-Za-z\.-]+$/
    end
  end

  newparam(:source) do
    desc 'Software installation http/https source.'
    newvalues(/https?:\/\//, /\//)
    #validate do |value|
    #  unless Pathname.new(value).absolute? ||
    #         URI.parse(value).is_a?(URI::HTTP)
    #    fail("Invalid source #{value}")
    #  end
    #end
  end

  newparam(:replace_config) do
    desc 'Whether config files should be overridden by package operations'
    defaultto :no
    newvalues(:yes, :no)
  end

  autorequire(:file) do
    self[:source] if self[:source] and Pathname.new(self[:source]).absolute?
  end

  # This has been commented out b/c it is just an example.
  # Because all providers will not have a source parameter, this validation
  # should be on the providers and not the type.
  # validate do
  #   fail('source is required when ensure is present')
  #   if self[:ensure] == :present and self[:source].nil?
  #end
end
```

Conclusion

This chapter covered the type API, walking through the process of creating an example type called `custom_package`. Although you can now create resource of this type in Puppet's DSL, the resource does not have a way to manage packages until it has a functional provider. In the next chapter, we will build upon our example and demonstrate how to implement multiple providers for this resource on a variety of platforms.

## CHAPTER 3

Providers

Providers implement the actions used to manage resources on a system. Where types express the interfaces used to describe resources, providers implement how resources interact with the underlying system. This clear separation between the interface and the implementation allows multiple providers to be specified for each type. The native type `package`, for example, has separate providers that can interact with package utilities across a large number of Linux systems, including `apt`, `yum`, `rpm`, and `zypper`.

In the last chapter, we created a type called `custom_package`, along with a list of attributes describing the resource. This type can be used to express packages that Puppet manages, like the following example:

```
custom_package { 'httpd':
  ensure  => present,
  version => '1.2.3-5',
}
```

This chapter will demonstrate how to implement multiple providers for our `custom_package` type and covers the following:

- How to create a custom provider and associate it with a type
- How Puppet determines the most appropriate provider
- How providers manage resource state
- How providers query for a list of all instances
- Provider optimizations

Creating a Provider

Because providers manage the system state described by a resource type, you must first retrieve the instance of a type associated with the provider. The `type` method can be called on `Puppet::Type` to access any instance of either a native or custom type that Puppet knows about.

 Many of the examples in this chapter will use *irb* to interact directly with Puppet through Ruby methods. This allows you to quickly dig into Puppet's APIs without having to write Ruby source files and Puppet manifests. The character >> indicates example code that is run interactively in *irb* and ⇒ indicates the value returned from an expression evaluated in *irb*.

The examples below show how to retrieve a type and associate a provider with it in *irb*.

```
>> require 'puppet'
>> Puppet::Type.type(:package)
=> Puppet::Type::Package
```

The `provide` method associates a provider with a specific type. The example below demonstrates how an `apt` provider is added to our example `custom_package` type from the last chapter:

```
>> require 'puppet'
>> Puppet.parse_config
>> Puppet::Type.type(:custom_package).provide(:apt)
=> Puppet::Type::Custom_package::ProviderApt
```

Custom providers are stored in a directory matching the name of the type with which they are associated. This directory is located in a module under the *lib/puppet/provider* folder. The name of the file should reflect the provider that is implemented. The following example shows the directory structure of a module that adds `apt`, `rpm` and `yum` providers to our custom_package type:

```
`-- lib
    `-- puppet
        |-- provider
        |   `-- custom_package
        |       |-- apt.rb
        |       `-- rpm.rb
        |       `-- yum.rb
        `-- type
            `-- custom_package.rb
```

The following template demonstrates how the full path of a provider is constructed:

```
<module_path>/<module_name>/lib/puppet/provider/<type_name>/<provider_name>.rb
```

Like types, providers must be located in the correct directory in order for Puppet to properly load them. When Puppet is running in agent/master mode, they must also be *pluginsync*ed to the agents.

The code below adds multiple providers for apt, rpm, and yum to our example type, custom_package:

```
# /etc/puppet/modules/example/lib/puppet/provider/custom_package/rpm.rb
Puppet::Type.type(:custom_package).provide(:rpm) do
end

# /etc/puppet/modules/example/lib/puppet/provider/custom_package/yum.rb
Puppet::Type.type(:custom_package).provide(:yum) do
end

# /etc/puppet/modules/example/lib/puppet/provider/custom_package/apt.rb
Puppet::Type.type(:custom_package).provide(:apt) do
end
```

By convention, provider names reflect the utility they use to interface with the system. For example, the providers above have been named after their package management commands.

You can call the providers method on an instance of a type to list all providers that have been associated with that type. This can be useful for figuring out if Puppet can properly locate your custom providers. The following example shows how to get a full list of all providers associated with Puppet's native type Package:

```
>>require 'puppet'
>>Puppet::Type.type(:package).providers
=> [:windows, :portage, :pkgin, :macports, :rpm, :appdmg, :aix, :up2date,
:ports, :pkgutil, :fink, :nim, :blastwave, :apt, :portupgrade, :yum, :pip,
:sun, :dpkg, :pkgdmg, :aptitude, :apple, :pkg, :msi, :freebsd, :sunfreeware,
:pacman, :zypper, :urpmi, :rug, :gem, :openbsd, :aptrpm, :hpux]
```

Now that we have demonstrated how to create providers and associate them with a corresponding type, the next sections will explain how they are implemented. When Puppet encounters a resource type, the first task is to iterate through all of the providers for that type, in order to determine which one is most appropriate for the current system.

Suitability

Because it is possible to have multiple providers for the same resource type, the provider API has three methods that determine which provider is most appropriate for a given system: `confine`, `defaultfor`, and `commands`. The `confine` and `commands` methods determine which providers are valid, and `defaultfor` indicates the default provider to use when there are multiple suitable providers.

confine

The `confine` method determines whether the current system applying a resource is capable of using a given provider. When processing a resource in the catalog, Puppet loads all of the providers for each resource type and uses `confine` to determine which providers are valid on the current system. A provider may specify multiple confines, and all conditions must be satisfied to deem the provider suitable.

This section will discuss confinement in detail, describing the different sources of information that Puppet can use to determine suitability: facts, files, features, or the boolean result of an arbitrary code block.

Fact confinement

The `confine` method can use Facter data collected from the current system to determine if a provider is valid. The `operatingsystem` fact is the most common source of information used for confinement, because providers are typically associated with a specific platform. The facts `kernel` and `osfamily` are also commonly used for provider confinement.

The `confine` method accepts a hash that maps the fact names to values that are used to indicate if a certain host is suitable for a provider:

```
confine :fact_name => :fact_value
```

The example below demonstrates how the `confine` method restricts a package provider to only Redhat-based distributions:

```
Puppet::Type.type(:custom_package).provide(:yum) do
  confine :operatingsystem => [:redhat, :fedora, :centos, :scientific]
end
```

The `osfamily` fact was introduced in Facter 1.5.7. The following example specifies multiple providers that are suitable for Redhat distros using the `osfamily` fact for confinement:

```
Puppet::Type.type(:custom_package).provide(:rpm) do
  confine :osfamily => :redhat
end
```

```
Puppet::Type.type(:custom_package).provide(:yum) do
  confine :osfamily => :redhat
end
```

In addition to facts, Puppet supports several other special confinement keys that determine suitability of providers.

File confinement

The `confine` method can use `exists` to base confinement on whether a specific file is present on the managed system.

The example below demonstrates how a provider managing the Puppet config file is restricted to systems where a valid Puppet configuration file already exists:

```
Puppet::Type.type(:puppet_config).provide(:ruby) do
  # Puppet[:config] varies depending on the account running puppet.
  # ~/.puppet/puppet.conf or /etc/puppet/puppet.conf
  confine :exists => Puppet[:config]
end
```

 All Puppet configuration settings are accessible by indexing the name of the setting as a symbol out of the Puppet hash. The *irb* example below shows how to interactively determine the values of a few settings (Puppet.parse_config is only required in Puppet ≥ 3.0):

```
> require 'puppet'
=> true
> Puppet.parse_config
=> ...
> Puppet[:config]
=> "/etc/puppetlabs/puppet/puppet.conf"
> Puppet[:vardir]
=> "/var/opt/lib/pe-puppet"
```

Feature confinement

Puppet provides a capability called *features*, which maintains a list of functionalities supported by the current system. This collection of features reflects the current Puppet run mode, the operating system type (POSIX vs. Windows), and whether specific libraries/software packages are installed on the system. Features are another supported criteria for confinement. The following features are available for provider confinement: `augeas`, `selinux`, `libshadow`, `root`, `ssh`, `microsoft_windows`, `posix`.

 The complete list of Puppet features is available in the following directory of Puppet's source code: *~/src/puppet/lib/puppet/feature/*.

This gem provider for our custom_package confines itself using Puppet's built-in :rubygems feature so that it is only suitable on systems where Ruby's package manager is installed:

```
Puppet::Type.type(:custom_package).provide(:gems) do
  confine :feature => :rubygems
end
```

Boolean confinement

confine also accepts :true and :false boolean values to restrict providers. This is the most flexible confinement method because it compares the return result of arbitrary executed code to :true or :false respectively.

The following code demonstrates a provider that can only be used if *puppet.conf* has an agent section:

```
Puppet::Type.type(:agent_config).provide(:parsed) do
  confine :exists => Puppet[:config]
  confine :true => begin
    if File.exists?(Puppet[:config])
      File.readlines(Puppet[:config]).find {|line|  line =~ /^\s*\[agent\]/ }
    end
  end
end
```

 The keywords begin and end are used to denote a block. The value returned by the block is the value of the last evaluated expression (just like a method). This allows us to pass a section of code without having to write a specific method for the boolean confinement.

defaultfor

confine is a convenient way to specify which providers are suitable for a given system, but it may still result in multiple valid providers for a resource type. In this situation, the type should specify its prefered provider with the defaultfor method.

This method accepts a fact name and value that are used to determine which provider is the default for certain types of systems:

```
defaultfor :fact_name => :fact_value
```

In our previous example, both the yum and rpm providers are valid for our custom_pack age type on Redhat systems. The defaultfor method can be used in conjunction with the operating system fact to specify that yum is the default provider for Redhat systems:

```
Puppet::Type.type(:custom_package).provide(:yum) do
  confine :osfamily => :redhat
  defaultfor :osfamily => :redhat
end
```

When multiple providers specify `defaultfor` and satisfy all confinement conditions, Puppet will pick the first suitable provider and log a warning. When developing providers, do not set `defaultfor` when there is no clear preferred choice among multiple providers. In these situations, Puppet users can explicitly request a specific provider by declaring the `provider` metaparameter in Puppet's DSL. This also permits users to override the default provider when the system supports more than one suitable provider.

Gem packages are a great example of this use case. Gem package management is confined to systems where `rubygems` are installed as indicated by the `rubygems` feature. However, gems would never be preferred as the default over the system's native package manager. Gems can only be managed by explicitly setting the provider as below:

```
package { 'json':
  ensure   => present,
  provider => 'gem',
}
```

Providers can also be confined based on whether certain commands are available in the current system PATH by using the `commands` method. This is covered in more detail in the next section, because it does much more than just confine a provider based on the availability of a command.

commands

Providers commonly interact with the underlying system by invoking command-line utilities. The *commands* method encapsulates a set of commands as Ruby methods available in the provider's definition. These dynamically created methods accept a list of arguments that are passed to the command line invocation. Providers (such as those for Puppet's file resource type and host resource type) can manage resources directly via Ruby APIs, but it is more common to interact via commands.

The `commands` method also confines providers based on the commands available when Puppet applies a resource. Any command specified using this method must be present in order for that provider to be used.

 Starting in Puppet 2.7.8, all confinement of providers in Puppet is "lazy," meaning that suitability for providers is determined the first time a resource of a type is evaluated. This means Puppet can install a package that makes a command available on the same run where it is used. Previously, the method `optional_commands` specified commands that are optional, but this is no longer necessary with lazy evaluation.

We can now specify the commands that are used by a few of our `custom_package` providers:

```
Puppet::Type.type(:custom_package).provide(:yum) do
  ...
  commands :rpm => 'rpm', :yum => 'yum'
end

Puppet::Type.type(:custom_package).provide(:apt) do
  ...
  commands :apt => 'apt', :dpkg => 'dpkg'
end
```

 When an absolute path is not specified, Puppet will search through each directory in the environment variable `$PATH` until the command is discovered. This is the preferred method for locating commands, since different operating systems may store commands in different directories and Puppet will detect them as long they are in the system load path. Fully qualified paths should only be used if the command is located in an unusual path that is not in the system default path, such as */opt/puppet/bin/gem* for the Puppet Enterprise bundled gem command instead of the system gem.

This example shows how to create a method called `apt_get` and use it to force install an `apt` package. The dash from the `apt-get` command is switched to an underscore because dashes are not allowed in Ruby method names:

```
Puppet::Type.type(:custom_package).provide(:apt) do
  ...
  commands :apt_get => "apt-get"
  ...
  def force_install_package(package_name = resource[:name])
    apt_get('install', '-f', package_name)
  end
  ...
end
```

Using the methods generated by `commands` has several advantages over Ruby's built-in methods for executing commands such as %x{*cmd*} or '*cmd*':

- Puppet displays all commands invoked from these methods when the `--debug` flag is set.

- Commands are documented as a requirement for the provider.

- The `Puppet::ExecutionFailure` exception is raised if the command has a non-zero exit code. This ensures that command failures are consistently handled throughout all providers.

Now that we have informed Puppet which commands are used to interact with the system, the next step is to implement the internals of our providers.

Properties and Providers

Previously, we discussed how Puppet's resource abstraction layer provides a clear separation between types and providers. Properties are the key to this separation. They describe the attributes of a resource that its providers are responsible for managing. For each property of a type, its providers are responsible for two actions:

- Retrieving the current state of that property
- Updating the resource state to match the desired state (as described by the resource)

Each of these actions is generally implemented as a single method per property.

In order to manage the state of our `custom_package` resource on the underlying system, Puppet must be able to do the following things:

1. Determine if a package is currently installed on the platform.
2. Discover the current version of the installed package.
3. Manage the state of the package by performing actions such as installation, removal, and upgrades.

This section will dive into the details of the provider methods that perform these actions, starting with a special property called `ensure` that handles resource creation and destruction.

ensure Property

`ensure` is a special property that models the existence of a resource. Until you implement `ensure`, resources cannot be created or destroyed. As we discussed in the previous chapter, invoking the `ensurable` method on a type adds the `ensure` property with the allowed values `absent` and `present`:

```
Puppet::Type.newtype(:custom_package) do
  ensurable
end
```

Now a resource of our type `custom_package` can be described as being absent or present. The value `present` on the `ensure` property indicates that the resource should be created if it does not already exist:

```
custom_package { 'httpd':
  ensure => present,
}
```

The value `absent` indicates that the resource should be destroyed if it already exists:

```
custom_user { 'dan':
  ensure => absent,
}
```

In order to support the `ensure` property, resource providers must be able to check if the resource already exists, create resources that do not exist, and destroy resources that already exist. This functionality is implemented with the following methods: `exists`, `create`, and `destroy`.

exists? method

The `exists?` method is used to retrieve the current `ensure` state of a resource. It returns a boolean value to express whether the resource is already present on the system.

 By convention, Ruby methods that end with *?* are expected to return either `true` or `false`.

In order to determine if a resource exists, the provider needs access to the resource's `namevar` and all attribute values used to declare that resource.

Providers responsible for managing the following resource need to know the package name (`httpd`) to determine if it exists:

```
custom_package { 'apache2':
  name   => 'httpd',
  ensure => present,
}
```

Any parameter can be retrieved via the `resource` method using the attribute name as the key. Each attribute can be indexed using the [] notation and supplying the name of the attribute to retrieve as a symbol. The example below uses `resource[:name]` to access the `namevar` of the package being managed. It passes this value to the `rpm` method created by the `commands` method to determine whether the package is installed:

```
Puppet::Type.type(:custom_package).provide(:yum) do
  confine :osfamily => :redhat
```

```
commands :yum => '/usr/bin/yum',
         :rpm => '/bin/rpm'

def exists?
  begin
    rpm('-q', resource[:name])
  rescue Puppet::ExecutionFailure => e
    false
  end
end
end
```

When Puppet applies an ensurable resource, it first checks the resource state by calling the exists? method. This method returns true to indicate that a resource already exists and false otherwise. In the example above, the command rpm -q <*package_name*> is executed by the exists? method to check if a package is installed. If the rpm command returns a non-zero exit code, it will raise a Puppet::ExecutionFailure exception. The exists? method explicitly catches this exception and returns false to indicate that the package is not installed.

Puppet compares the result of the exists? method with the declared value of the ensure property to determine the next method(s) to invoke.

Creating/Destroying Resources

The create and destroy methods modify a resource's existence state according to the user's declaration. create will only be invoked when the ensure state of a resource has been set as present, and the exists? method returns false (indicating that the resource does not exist). The destroy method will only be invoked when the ensure state of a resource has been set as absent, and the exists? method returns true (indicating that the resource exists).

Table 3-1 shows how Puppet compares the results from the exists? method to the value of the ensure property to determine what action the provider takes:

Table 3-1. Comparisons based on exists? method results

exists? method result	ensure value	Action	ensure state transition
true	present	manage other properties	n/a
true	absent	destroy method	present → absent
false	present	create method	absent → present
false	absent	do nothing	n/a

As indicated in Table 3-1, properties other than ensure are only individually managed when ensure is set to present and the resource already exists. When a resource state is absent, Puppet ignores any specified resource property.

Resources should have all of their properties configured correctly upon creation. Puppet assumes resources will be created with the correct properties. The methods managing individual properties of a resource are not invoked when create is called. When the create method is implemented incorrectly, it results in two Puppet runs for resources to reach their desired state; one to first create the resource, then again to sync the resource properties. This is why the create method for the yum provider below appends the specified version to the package name before performing the installation:

```
Puppet::Type.type(:custom_package).provide(:yum) do
  confine :osfamily => :redhat

  commands :yum => '/usr/bin/yum',
           :rpm => '/bin/rpm'

  def exists?
    begin
      rpm('-q', resource[:name])
      true
    rescue Puppet::ExecutionFailure => e
      false
    end
  end

  def create
    package= resource[:version] ? "#{resource[:name]}-#{resource[:version]}" :
resource[:name]
    yum('install', '-y', package)
  end

  def destroy
    yum('erase', '-y', resource[:name])
  end

end
```

After implementing supporting methods for an ensurable resource, it is important to verify the resource is working correctly with puppet resource. Be sure to comment out the version property from the type we developed in the last section because we have not implemented its corresponding provider methods yet.

Now you can use puppet resource to create a custom_package resource:

```
$ puppet resource custom_package httpd ensure=present --debug
debug: Puppet::Type::Custom_package::ProviderYum: Executing '/bin/rpm -q httpd'
```

```
debug: Puppet::Type::Custom_package::ProviderYum:
  Executing '/usr/bin/yum install httpd'
notice: /Custom_package[httpd]/ensure changed 'absent' to 'present'
debug: Finishing transaction -607733468
debug: Storing state
debug: Stored state in 0.04 seconds
custom_package { 'httpd':
  ensure => 'present',
}
```

You can also use Puppet to destroy the same package:

```
$ puppet resource custom_package httpd ensure=absent --debug
```

Now that we have implemented the `ensure` property for our `custom_package` type, let's move on to implementing the `version` property methods. If the package already exists on the system and `ensure` is set to `present`, Puppet will obtain the package version via the `version` method. It compares the current version to the user-declared value to decide if the `version=` method should also be called. The following section will cover how to implement those two methods.

Managing Properties

Puppet does much more than just manage the existence of resources. The provider should implement two methods which get and set values for each property. When a declared resource already exists, Puppet invokes these methods to manage individual properties. First, Puppet calls the getter method to retrieve the current value, then Puppet compares the result against the user-declared value and conditionally invokes a setter method to update the value.

Our package resource supports a property called `version` that was added to the type with the following code:

```
Puppet::Type.newtype(:custom_package) do
  ...
  newproperty(:version) do
  end
end
```

The method retrieving the version value matches the property name, where the method setting the value is appended with `=(value)`:

```
...
def version
  # implement the command to obtain package version.
end
```

```
def version=(value)
  # implement the command to install a specific package version
end
...
```

You can now implement getters and setters for your yum provider to set a package to an exact version:

```
Puppet::Type.type(:custom_package).provide('yum') do

  commands :yum => '/usr/bin/yum',
           :rpm => '/bin/rpm'

  def version
    version = rpm('-q', resource[:name])
    if version =~ /^#{Regexp.escape(resource[:name])}-(.*)/
      $1
    end
  end

  def version=(value)
    yum('install', "#{resource[:name]}-#{resource[:version]}")
  end
  ...
end
```

The version=(value) method is a naive implementation that does not handle downgrade properly. The correct implementation should compare against the installed software version and invoke package downgrade when appropriate. The code here is kept simple; for more complete examples, see the ~/src/puppet/lib/puppet/provider/packages directory.

When all the resource properties have the appropriate provider methods implemented, you can execute puppet resource to manage the resource:

```
$ puppet resource custom_package mysql
custom_package { 'mysql':
  ensure => present,
  version => '5.0.95-1.el5_7.1',
}
```

At this point, you have a fully functional puppet resource. However, the implementation isn't finished because the command puppet resource custom_package doesn't show a list of packages. The next section will discuss how to implement the ability to query for all resource instances for a given provider.

Discovering and Prefetching Resources

So far, we have only discussed how providers manage resources by configuring the system state to match their declared state. Puppet supports an additional mode of operation: the discovery of resources. This retrieves the current state of all resources of a given type on a system.

This section introduces the `self.instances` method and demonstrates how it enables providers to discover resource instances of a specific type on the current system. We will also discuss `self.prefetch`, which is used to cache the state of all managed resources of a given type in the catalog.

It is important to understand Puppet command line invocations that operate by discovering versus managing resources, because this determines whether Puppet invokes `self.instances` or `self.prefetch`. Table 3-2 shows which of these methods is invoked for commonly used Puppet actions.

Table 3-2. Comparing discovery vs. prefetching actions

Command	Provider method	Mode
puppet apply	self.prefetch	management
puppet agent	self.prefetch	management
puppet resource <type>	self.instances	discovery
puppet resource <type> <title>	self.instances	discovery
puppet resource <type> <title> <attr1=value1>	self.prefetch	management

This section will discuss how to implement `self.instances` for your providers to support querying for resources with `puppet resource`. We will also discuss how `self.prefetch` and `self.instances` work in conjunction to improve the provider's performance when applying a catalog.

Discovery with self.instances

The `self.instances` method returns all instances of a resource type that its provider finds on the current system. Implementing this method allows the `puppet resource` command to query the system for instances of that type and return a list of resources in the command line.

 Provider methods whose name are prefixed with "self" are invoked when the type is being initialized and not when individual resources are managed. These methods are called once per provider, as opposed to the other provider methods we have seen so far, which are called for each resource being managed.

Figure 3-1 illustrates which methods are called per provider versus per resource for our `custom_package`'s providers.

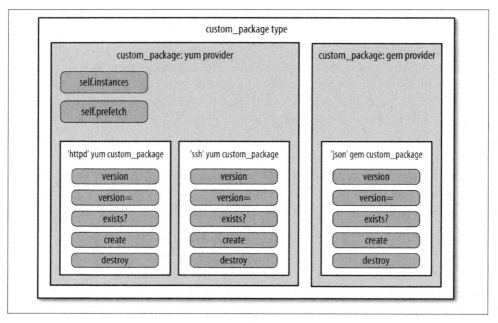

Figure 3-1. custom_package type with yum and gem providers

The example below shows how to use `rpm -qa` to query for a list of all packages that our providers can discover on a Redhat system:

```
def self.instances
  packages = rpm('-qa','--qf','%{NAME} %{VERSION}-%{RELEASE}\n')
  packages.split("\n").collect do |line|
    name, version = line.split(' ', 2)
    new( :name   => name,
      :ensure => :present,
      :version => version
    )
  end
end
```

The `self.instances` method returns an array of the discovered resources. In the example above, these resources are created by calling the method `new` for each package and passing its properties as a hash. `ensure` is set explicitly to `:present` in this hash because all resources discovered by `rpm -qa` are assumed to exist on the current system. All attributes set in this hash are assigned to the resource's property hash, which will be covered in the next section.

The Property Hash

Each resource returned by the `self.instances` method stores its discovered attributes in an instance variable called `@property_hash`. This hash keys are the cached properties that were explicitly passed to the `new` method. In our `yum` provider example, the `:name`, `:ensure`, and `:version` attributes can all be referenced out of the `@proper ty_hash` using a symbol as the index (i.e., `@property_hash[:version]`).

Any provider method can access values from the property hash. The example below demonstrates how to simplify the `exists?` and `version` methods for our provider with the values cached in the `@property_hash`:

```
...
def self.instances
  packages = rpm('-qa','--qf','%{NAME} %{VERSION}-%{RELEASE}\n')
  packages.split("\n").collect do |line|
    name, version = line.split(' ', 2)
    # initializes @property_hash
    new( :name    => name,
            :ensure => :present,
            :version => version
    )
  end
end
...
def exists?
  @property_hash[:ensure] == :present
end

def version
  @property_hash[:version]
end
...
```

The source code above will only work for `puppet resource` query commands. The `@property_hash` will not be initialized correctly for other commands until we implement `self.prefetch`, which will be covered in a later section.

The `self.instances` method should only cache the values of properties if they are discovered as part of the process for finding existing resources. If the property value was not collected by `self.instances`, Puppet will still invoke the property's getter methods to obtain their value.

Resource properties that require additional commands should be implemented in their respective getter method. For example, the `show databases` command returns a list of databases on a mysql server, but the results do not contain individual properties, such as character encoding. The retrieval of character encoding should be performed in the property's getter method, because this method will only be called for databases Puppet manages. This avoids the unnecessary request for encoding information on unmanaged databases.

Query All Resources

Now that we've implemented `self.instances` and modified our getter methods (`version` and `exists?`) to use the `@property_hash`, we can finally query for all instances of yum custom_packages with `puppet resource`:

```
$ puppet resource custom_package
custom_package { 'acl':
  ensure  => 'present',
  version => '2.2.39-8.el5',
}
custom_package { 'acpid':
  ensure  => 'present',
  version => '1.0.4-12.el5',
}
custom_package { 'alsa-lib':
  ensure  => 'present',
  version => '1.0.17-1.el5',
}
custom_package { 'amtu':
  ensure  => 'present',
  version => '1.0.6-2.el5',
}
...
```

 Puppet queries for resource instances across all suitable providers. The example in this section assumes there is only one suitable provider for our custom_package type. Puppet will fail to query resources if any of the suitable providers have not implemented `self.instances`. For this reason, many providers in Puppet's source code simply return `[]` from self.instances.

```
def self.instances
  []
end
```

Adding the `--debug` flag to the command above shows that the previous example retrieves the state of all packages on the system with a single system call, `rpm -qa`:

```
$ puppet resource custom_package --debug
debug: Puppet::Type::Custom_package::ProviderYum:
  Executing '/bin/rpm -qa --qf %{NAME} %{VERSION}-%{RELEASE}\n'
```

```
custom_package { 'acl':
  ensure  => 'present',
  version => '2.2.39-8.el5',
}
```

This also allows you to query for the current state of a specific `custom_package` resource:

```
$ puppet resource custom_package acl
custom_package { 'acl':
  ensure  => 'present',
  version => '2.2.39-8.el5',
}
```

Once `self.instances` has been implemented, you can use it directly from *irb* to query for all instances of a resource type. The example below demonstrates how you can use `self.instances` to query for a list of all Puppet Enterprise packages that are installed using Puppet's built-in package type:

```
>> require 'puppet'
>> require 'pp'
# get all packages from the system
>> packages = Puppet::Type.type(:package).instances
# filter for packages whose name starts with pe
>> pe_packages = packages.select{|resource| resource.name =~ /^pe/ }
# transform the list of resources into hashes
>> pe_packages.collect {|p| { p.to_hash  }
```

Now that you have seen how `self.instances` retrieves the current state of all `yum custom_package` resources using a single command, we can discuss how the same principle can be used to optimize our providers by prefetching the state of all managed resources with a single system call.

Prefetching Managed Resources

When managing resources, the `self.prefetch` method is invoked the first time that Puppet encounters a given resource type. It provides a hook for programming logic that is always performed before any resources of that type are applied. This is typically used to cache or "prefetch" the state of all resource instances that a given provider can discover.

Providers that are capable of performing a single inexpensive lookup to retrieve the state of all resources on the system should implement this method. In Puppet, the file type's providers do not implement `self.instances` or `self.prefetch` because the operations required to list all files on a system are prohibitively expensive. Imagine how slow management of files would be if you had to query for the state of all files on the system just to set the mode of a single file!

The `prefetch` method accepts an argument that is a hash of all managed resources of the provider's type. It is commonly used in conjunction with `self.instances` to populate the property hash for those resources.

The example below shows `self.prefetch` setting the provider (which contains the property hash) for all managed resources by invoking `self.instances` (i.e., `instances`):

```
def self.prefetch(resources)
  packages = instances
  resources.keys.each do |name|
    if provider = packages.find{ |pkg| pkg.name == name }
      resources[name].provider = provider
    end
  end
end
```

The code above does the following:

1. Discovers all `custom_package` resources on the system by invoking `self.instances`.

2. Iterates through all custom_package resources in the catalog.

3. If the managed package exists in the `self.instances` cache, assigns its provider to set its property hash.

The example below shows how to implement our `yum` provider with `self.instances` and prefetching. This allows the state of all resources and properties to be queried by this provider with a single system call to `rpm -qa`:

```
Puppet::Type.type(:custom_package).provide('yum') do
  ...
  def self.instances
    packages = rpm('-qa','--qf','%{NAME} %{VERSION}-%{RELEASE}\n')
    packages.split("\n").collect do |line|
      name, version = line.split
      new( :name => name,
           :ensure => :present,
           :version => version,
      )
    end
  end

  def self.prefetch(resources)
    packages = instances
    resources.keys.each do |name|
      if provider = packages.find{ |pkg| pkg.name == name }
        resources[name].provider = provider
      end
    end
  end

  def exists?
    @property_hash[:ensure] == :present
  end
```

```
def version
  @property_hash[:version]
end
...
end
```

 Query actions will fail if self.instances is not defined for a provider while manage actions will only invoke self.prefetch when it is defined. If self.instance is implemented but the self.prefetch method is omitted, the commands puppet agent, puppet apply will not populate each resource's @property_hash. An empty @property_hash in the example code above returns incorrect values for the exists? and version methods, resulting in incorrectly retrieved resource states.

We recommend using self.prefetch to populate the property hash when it is possible to discover all your resources with a single command. When collecting resources requires multiple commands, implementing self.prefetch may detract from instead of increase performance. For example, if each service status requires a separate system call (*service <service_name> status*), then prefetching should not be enabled for services. In short: Puppet should not indiscriminately query every service's status on the system just to manage a subset of the possible services.

Resource attribute values should be prefetched into the @property_hash when appropriate. This simplifies property methods for the provider and Puppet provides a shortcut to autogenerate them, called mk_resource_methods.

Generated Property Methods

When you implement self.instances and self.prefetch, all attribute getters retrieve their values from the property hash if they were cached. This results in an excessive amount of repetitive provider code for resource types with a large number of properties. Puppet provides the convenience method mk_resource_methods that dynamically generates getter methods for each resource property by retrieving their values from the property hash.

The example below comments out the code that is generated by mk_resource_methods:

```
mk_resource_methods

# generates the following methods via Ruby metaprogramming
# def version
#   @property_hash[:version] || :absent
# end
```

You can explicitly override the methods created by `mk_resource_methods` by implementing a method of the same name. This allows you to take advantage of autogenerating attribute methods via `mk_resource_methods`, while still retaining the flexibility to implement custom property methods that do not conform to this simple pattern.

Managing a Resource

The `puppet resource` command is able to manage resources as long as their setter methods (`create`, `destroy`, and `version=`) are implemented for our `custom_package`'s `yum` provider:

```
...
def create
  if resource[:version]
   yum('install', '-y', "#{resource[:name]}-#{resource[:version]}")
  else
    yum('install', '-y', resoure[:name])
  end
end

def destroy
  yum('erase', resource[:name])
end
...
def version=(value)
  yum('install', "#{resource[:name]}-#{resource[:version]}")
end
...
```

The command below demonstrates how you can use `puppet resource` to manage the `ensure` state of your custom_package:

```
$ puppet resource custom_package httpd ensure=present
notice: /Custom_package[httpd]/ensure: created
custom_package { 'httpd':
  ensure => 'absent',
}
```

The output above indicates an event resulting in the creation of the `httpd` package, but the returned resource hash indicates the `httpd` `custom_package` is absent. This is because Puppet determines the state of this resource based on the value returned by the `exists?` method which relies on the value cached in the property hash. This means that any methods that modify the resource's state need to update the @property_hash to reflect those changes. This ensures that the `puppet resource` command shows the correct value when Puppet modifies the system state.

The example below demonstrates how to update your setter methods to keep the property hash up-to-date with the system changes they make:

```
...
def create
  if resource[:version]
    yum('install', '-y', "#{resource[:name]}-#{resource[:version]}")
  else
    yum('install', '-y', resoure[:name])
  end
  @property_hash[:ensure] = :present
end

def destroy
  yum('erase', resource[:name])
  @property_hash.clear
end
...
def version=(value)
  yum('install', "#{resource[:name]}-#{resource[:version]}")
  @property_hash[:version] = value
end
...
```

Once these methods have been refactored, the output of puppet resource will indicate the current state of resources that are modified:

```
$ puppet resource custom_package httpd ensure=present
notice: /Custom_package[httpd]/ensure: created
custom_package { 'httpd':
  ensure => 'present',
}
```

The previous example only updates the property hash after the yum command has executed successfully. If you update the property hash before that command, a command failure would result in a property hash that is not consistent with the current system state.

Flush

The flush method provides a hook for logic that should be executed after all properties of a resources have been applied. This is typically used to improve performance by synchronizing multiple properties with a single call. If defined, the flush method is always invoked once per resource when any property changes. It relies on the data supplied by a resource's setter methods to determine what properties it needs to synchronize.

Previously, we demonstrated how to implement setter methods to update the state of individual properties. For providers with a large number of properties, this can lead to large numbers of interactions with the underlying system.

For example, a `custom_user` resource could implement multiple properties using the `usermod` command in the setter method of each of those properties:

```
...
def uid=(value)
  usermod('-u', value, resource[:name])
end

def gid=(value)
  usermod('-g', value, resource[:name])
end

def shell=(value)
  usermod('-s', value, resource[:name])
end
```

With the provider implementation above, it could take upwards of three separate system calls to synchronize a `custom_user`. Rather than invoking the `usermod` command for every property change, you can simply update the system once with the `flush` method to improve performance.

The example above can be reimplemented to use `flush` as follows:

```
...
def initialize(value={})
  super(value)
  @property_flush = {}
end

def uid=(value)
  @property_flush[:uid] = value
end

def gid=(value)
  @property_flush[:gid] = value
end

def shell=(value)
  @property_flush[:shell] = value
end

def flush
  options = []
    if @property_flush
    (options << '-u' << resource[:uid])   if @property_flush[:uid]
    (options << '-g' << resource[:gid])   if @property_flush[:gid]
    (options << '-s' << resource[:shell]) if @property_flush[:shell]
    unless options.empty?
      usermod(options, resource[:name]) unless options.empty?
```

```
        end
    end
    @property_hash = resource.to_hash
  end
```

Notice that the above example initializes an instance variable `@property_flush`. The desired value of all properties that need to be updated are stored in this hash. The `flush` method synchronizes the state of all of these properties using a single call to `usermod` with the updated values of the property hash. Also note that `flush` ensures that the `@property_hash` in our example is always set to be the same as the declared resource.

Unlike property-specific methods that are invoked conditionally based on resource state, the `flush` method will always be invoked at the end whether Puppet is creating, destroying, or modifying the resource. Our example above needs to add extra conditional logic to ensure that `useradd` is only called if `create` or `destroy` was not invoked (if either of these methods is invoked, then options will be empty).

 When using the `flush` method, logged events do not necessarily indicate that something has changed, they merely indicate that changes have been queued up in our `property_flush` hash. When Puppet's execution is interrupted, events may be reported that were not committed by the `flush` method.

By default, Puppet synchronizes properties in the order they are declared in the resource type. For complex resources where the property updates need to follow a specific sequence, the `flush` method can also be used to issue several commands in the precise order required to update the resource properly.

Purging Resources

Implementing the `self.instances` method automatically enables purging for ensurable types. Purging ensures that only resources explicitly declared in Puppet's catalog are allowed to exist on a system; all other resources will be removed from the system.

You can enable purging for a resource type using the `resources` resource (yes, that really is the name of it):

```
resources { 'custom_package':
  purge => true,
}
```

Purging is not very common for packages because of the large number of packages on a system. It is extremely useful, however, for other resources such as hosts:

```
host { 'localhost':
  ensure => present,
  ip     => '127.0.0.1',
}
resources { 'host':
  purge => true,
}
```

The above example purges all resources out of */etc/hosts* except a single localhost entry.

Implementing self.instances allows you to query for all instances of a resource, improves the performance of managing resources by drastically reducing the amount of system calls made, and enables purging. For these reasons, we recommend that you implement caching for resource providers that are capable of querying for all resource instances on a system.

Putting It All Together

Now that we have covered all of the details for how Puppet manages resource properties, we can walk through the process of how Puppet applies a catalog:

1. Converts the catalog into an ordered list of resources to apply.

2. Verifies that these declared resources conform to the type interface by calling the validate and munge methods of the type.

3. Invokes the prefetch method to cache values in the property hash if it was defined for the provider.

4. For each of those resources that is ensurable, Puppet first invokes the exists method to determine if that resource exists.

5. Compares the results of this method to the desired resource state.

6. Invokes create or destroy if the ensure state was not already in sync.

7. If the resource already existed, Puppet retrieves a list of its properties that were declared and iterates through them. For each property, it calls the default getter method and compares the value to the declared value. It finally calls the setter method if the values were not equal.

8. Invokes flush for each resource if the method is defined.

Conclusion

This chapter covered how to use Puppet's provider APIs to add multiple providers to our custom_package example. You should now be able to write fully functional and optimized providers that can manage and query puppet resources. The next chapter covers advanced capabilities that can be implemented in types and providers.

## CHAPTER 4

Advanced Types and Providers

The previous chapters covered the core concepts required to write fully functional types and providers. In this chapter, we will explore several advanced features and their implementation. These topics are not required for all custom types, but they have been included to ensure users have a more complete understanding of how Puppet works. Many of Puppet's native types provide the following functionalities and this chapter will cover how to implement them:

- Resources can respond to refresh events triggered by the notify/subscribe metaparameters.
- Providers may indicate they only support a subset of the functionality of a type interface.
- Types can customize the output of event messages.

The chapter also discusses how code can be shared between multiple providers using both provider inheritance as well as common shared libraries. Code reuse can simplify providers, and reduce the total amount of code that needs to be written and maintained, especially when you need multiple related providers for the same service.

After reading this chapter, you should be able to understand and implement:

- Supporting refresh signals initiated from the *subscribe/notify* metaparameter
- How providers can support a subset of a type's *features*
- Code reuse through parent providers and shared libraries
- Modifying event log messages

Refresh

In Puppet, when any properties are updated, an event is recorded which can trigger updates to other resources with a *refresh* signal. These special relationships are defined with the notify and subscribe metaparameters. This adds a *refresh* dependency between resources in addition to a regular order dependency (notify implies before, and subscribe implies require). This section will discuss how to implement the refresh method so a resource can respond to a refresh signal.

The most common usage of refresh relationships in Puppet is to trigger service restarts. When updating application settings, configuration file changes often require service restarts. The following demonstrates how an sshd custom_service can subscribe to changes in its configuration file:

```
file { '/etc/sshd.conf':
  content => template('ssh/sshd.conf.erb'),
}
custom_service { 'sshd':
  ensure => running,
  subscribe => File['/etc/sshd.conf'],
}
```

The sshd custom service in this example receives a refresh signal for any changes to the */etc/sshd.conf* file. Its type needs to implement the refresh method to respond to these signals, or any refresh signal will simply be ignored. In this case, notify or sub scribe simply indicate an ordering relationship and the refresh signal is ignored.

The example below implements the refresh method for the custom_service type. This method instructs the type to call the current provider's restart method when it receives a refresh signal and the ensure state of the resource was specified as :running:

```
Puppet::Type.newtype(:custom_service) do
  ...
  def refresh
    if (@parameters[:ensure] == :running)
      provider.restart
    else
      debug "Skipping restart; service is not running"
    end
  end
end
```

We also need to implement the provider's restart method invoked by the type's refresh method:

```
Puppet::Type.type(:custom_service).provide('service') do

  commands :service => 'service'
  ...
  def restart
```

```
      service(resource[:name], 'restart')
  end
  ...
end
```

Now, `custom_service` resources will be restarted when they receive refresh signals. The next section will discuss how to create providers that only support a subset of the functionality of its type using the `features` method.

Features

A single resource type can have multiple provider backends. In some cases, a provider may not support all functionalities described in the resource type. The `features` method allows the type to specify properties that will only be implemented by a subset of its providers. The providers can ignore feature specific properties unless they offer management for those functionalities and declare support for them. Unlike properties, parameters do not need to label feature support, since providers that do not support a parameter can simply ignore them.

For example, a database resource may have both MySQL and PostgreSQL backends. MySQL tables have the option of selecting a storage engine such as MyISAM, InnoDB, and memory (among several other choices). PostgreSQL does not offer this option since it only offers the built-in storage engine. In this case, the storage engine attribute should be labeled as a feature since it is only supported by one of the products. A single resource type can have multiple provider backends. In some cases, a provider does not support all functionalities described in the resource type. For example, a database resource may have both MySQL and PostgreSQL backend. In this case, the storage engine attribute should be labeled as a feature since it is only supported by one of the products. The `features` method allows the type to specify properties that require a unique functionality. The providers can ignore feature specific properties unless they support management for those functionalities and declare support for them. Unlike properties, parameters do not need to label feature support, since providers that do not support a parameter can simply ignore them.

A type declares the list of optional functionalities using the `feature` method with the following three arguments:

1. The name of the feature

2. Documentation for the feature

3. A list of methods a provider should implement to support a feature

The syntax for creating a feature is shown below:

```
feature :feature_name, "documentation on feature.",
  :methods => [:additional_method]
```

In our `custom_package` type from the last chapter, we implemented a property called `version`. This property is only supported by the subset of providers that have a notion of package versions. The following example demonstrates how a feature, `:versiona ble`, can be added to our `custom_package` type, and how our `version` property can indicate that it is only supported by providers that are versionable:

```
Puppet::Type.newtype(:custom_package) do
  ...
  feature :versionable, "Package manager interrogate and return software
    version."

  newproperty(:version, :required_features => :versionable) do
    ...
  end
end
```

Note that we did not specify a list of methods that are implemented by a provider to indicate that it supports this feature. When no methods are listed, a provider must explicitly declare its support for its feature with the `has_feature` method:

```
Puppet::Type.type(:custom_package).provide('yum') do
  has_feature :versionable
end
```

For `custom_package` providers that do not support versions, simply omit `has_fea ture :versionable`, and the property can be safely ignored. When Puppet encounters providers that do not support a specific feature or providers that are missing the required methods for a feature, it skips properties that depend on those features.

Code Reuse

There are a few ways in which common code can be shared between providers. Sharing code between providers is extremely useful because it reduces duplicate code across all providers. This section will discuss how providers can reuse code from parent providers and shared utility libraries.

Parent Providers

It is possible for multiple providers to use the same commands to perform a subset of their functionality. Providers are allowed a single parent provider. Providers reuse their parent's methods by default, and can optionally implement methods to override the parent's behavior.

A provider sets its parent by passing the `:parent` option to the `provide` method. The following trivial example shows how a Puppet Enterprise gem provider could reuse all of the existing functionality of the current gem provider and just update the path of the gem executable:

```
Puppet::Type.type(:package).provide :pe_gem, :parent => :gem do

  commands :gemcmd => "/opt/puppet/bin/gem"
end
```

The yum and rpm providers that we crafted in the last chapter can use provider inheritance to share most of their functionality. Since the yum provider relies on rpm for retrieving the current state of packages on the system, it can use inheritance to avoid having to reimplement these methods. The following example is the rpm provider which will be the parent provider for yum:

```
Puppet::Type.type(:custom_package).provide(:rpm) do
  commands :rpm => 'rpm'
  mkresource_method

  self.prefetch
    packages = rpm('-qa','--qf','%{NAME} %{VERSION}-%{RELEASE}\n')
    packages.split("\n").collect do |line|
      name, version = line.split
      new( :name => name,
           :ensure => :present,
           :version => version,
      )
    end
  end

  self.instances
    packages = instances
    resources.keys.each do |name|
      if provider = packages.find{ |pkg| pkg.name == name }
        resources[name].provider = provider
      end
    end
  end

  def exists?
    @property_hash[:ensure] == :present
  end

  def create
    fail "RPM packages require source parameter" unless resource[:source]
    rpm('-iU', resource[:source])
    @property_hash[:ensure] = :present
  end

  def destroy
    rpm('-e', resource[:name])
    @property_hash[:ensure] = :absent
  end
end
```

The provider above already implements several of the exact methods that our `yum` provider needs, namely: `self.instances`, `self.prefetch`, and `exists?`. The example below demonstrates how our `yum` provider can set its parent to the `rpm` provider and override that provider's `create` and `destroy` methods:

```
Puppet::Type.type(:custom_package).provide(:yum, :parent => :rpm) do
  commands :yum => 'yum'
  commands :rpm => 'rpm'

  def create
    if resource[:version]
      yum('install', '-y', "#{resource[:name]}-#{resource[:version]}")
    else
      yum('install', '-y', resoure[:name])
    end
    @property_hash[:ensure] = :present
  end

  def destroy
    yum('erase', resource[:name])
    @property_hash[:ensure] = :absent
  end
end
```

 A child provider does not currently share commands with its parent provider. Commands specified in the parent need to be specified again in the child using the `commands` methods.

Ruby extensions can share common code without using parent providers. Types and Providers occasionally need to share common libraries. The next section will discuss the conventions and challenges with sharing common code in custom Ruby extensions.

Shared Libraries

Puppet Labs recommends that utility code located in modules be stored in the following namespace: *lib/puppet_x/<organization>/*. Utility code should never be stored in *lib/puppet* because this may lead to unintended conflicts with puppet's source code, or with the source code from other providers.

The following directory tree contains an example module with two types, each of which has one provider. It also contains a class with some helper methods.

```
`-- lib
    |-- puppet
    |   |-- provider
    |   |   `-- one
    |   |       `-- default.rb
```

```
|    |       `-- two
|    |              `-- default.rb
|    `-- type
|        |-- one.rb
|        `-- two.rb
`-- puppet_x
     `-- bodeco
          `-- helper.rb
```

 For more information on this convention, see its Puppet Labs project
issue, #14149 (*http://projects.puppetlabs.com/issues/14149*).

Let's create a helper method shared among both providers:

```
class Puppet::Puppet_X::Bodeco::Helper
  def self.make_my_life_easier
  ...
  end
end
```

All code in a module's lib directory is *pluginsync*ed to agents along with types and providers. This does not, however, mean that all Ruby code in a module's *lib* directory will
automatically be available in Ruby's LOADPATH.

Due to limitations around how Puppet currently handles Ruby libraries, code should
only be shared within the same module, and then it should only be used by requiring
the relative path to the file. The provider should require the library as follows:

```
require File.expandpath(File.join(File.dirname(__FILE__), '..', '..', , '..',
'puppet_x', 'bodeco', 'helper.rb'))
Puppet::Type.type(:one).provide(:default) do

  def exists?
    Puppet::Puppet_X::Helper.make_my_life_easier
  end

end
```

The `require` method above should be explained in a little more detail:

1. FILE provides the full path of the current file being processed.

2. `File.dirname` is invoked in the full path of this file to return its directory name.

3. `File.join` is used to append the relative path *../../../puppet_x/bodeco* to our current
   directory path.

4. `File.expand_path` is used to convert the relative path into an absolute path.

The result of these methods is a relative path lookup for the helper utility in our current module. This relative path lookup is not recommended across modules, since modules can exist in different module directories that are both part of the current modulepath.

Customizing Event Output

Whenever Puppet modifies a resource, an event is recorded. The event message can be customized per resource attribute by overriding the should_to_s, is_to_s, and change_to_s methods.

When executing Puppet, if the current state of the resource does not match the resource specified desired state, Puppet will display the following log message:

```
notice: /#{resource_type}[#{resource_title}]/#{resource_attribute}:
    current_value 'existing_value', should be 'desired_value' (noop)
```

The output displayed for the current value is determined by calling is_to_s on the retrieved value of the resource. The value for the desired value is determined by calling should_to_s on the munged property value.

By default, Puppet simply transforms the attribute value to a string with Ruby's built-in method to_s. For hash values, this results in an incomprehensible string output. The following *irb* snippet shows what happens when you call to_s on a hash:

```
>> {'hello'=>'world'}.to_s
=> "helloworld"
```

If the property returns this hash value, the Puppet notice message would be "should be 'helloworld'". We can use the should_to_s and is_to_s methods as follows to override how hashes are displayed in Puppet's output:

```
newproperty(:my_hash) do
  def should_to_s(value)
     value.inspect
  end

  def is_to_s(value)
     value.inspect
  end
end
```

Now when the resource changes, the message is much more readable:

```
notice: ... : current_value '{"hello"=>"world"}', should be
  '{"goodbye"=>"world"}'
```

Usually, updating these methods to .inspect will provide sufficiently readable output, but in some cases where the attribute contains a long list of array values, it's helpful to display the differences rather than list all values. In these situations, the change_to_s method provides the flexibility to format this output:

```
newproperty(:my_array) do
  def change_to_s(current, desire)
    "removing #{(current-desire).inspect},
      adding #{(desire-current).inspect}."
  end
end
```

For hashes, there's rubygems `hashdiff`, which will show the differences between two
hashes:

```
require 'rubygems'
require 'hashdiff'

newproperty(:my_array) do
  def change_to_s(current, desire)
    "removing #{(HashDiff.diff(current,desire).inspect},
      adding #{HashDiff.diff(desire, current).inspect}."
  end
end
```

Now What?

This book covered the types and providers APIs used to implement custom resources.
With this knowledge, you should understand when and why—as well as how—to write
native resource types. We certainly have not explored every possible API call used by
Puppet's native types. Some were ignored on purpose because they are fairly complex
and we do not advocate using them, while others were omitted because the value of
using them is not clear, even to us.

For the more adventurous readers, the Puppet source code contains examples of every
possible supported API call: *lib/puppet/{type,provider,property}.rb*. In fact, we often used
Puppet's source code as a reference to ensure that concepts were correctly explained for
this book.

For new Puppet developers, the following resources are available for continued
assistance:

* The google puppet-dev mailing list (*http://groups.google.com/group/puppet-dev*)
* The Freenode IRC channels #puppet and #puppet-dev

Installing Puppet

The book assumes that users have installed Facter and Puppet from source in their *~/src* directory.

This section walks through the process of installing the following:

- Ruby
- Facter and Puppet

Installing Ruby

In general, Linux distributions provide Ruby 1.8.7, which can be installed as a system package. Earlier versions of Ruby 1.8 should be avoided due to performance issues and known bugs. Puppet 3.0 officially supports Ruby 1.9.x series—however, it is only available on the latest distributions.

 As of the publication date of this book, using Puppet 3.0 with Ruby 1.9.3 contains enough known issues that it should be avoided. This is likely to be fixed in the near future.

The following commands are sufficient for installing ruby and rubygems on Redhat- and Debian-based systems:

```
$ apt-get install ruby rubygems
$  yum install ruby rubygems
```

Installing Ruby from a package is sufficient if you only need to support a single Ruby environment. RVM is recommended for more complicated setups and in general for development with Ruby. It allows multiple versions of Ruby to be installed on the same system, and provides the ability to isolate specific sets of gems to different environments using gemsets. More information on RVM can be found here (*https://rvm.io/*).

```
curl -L https://get.rvm.io | bash -s stable --ruby

rvm install 1.8.7
rvm install 1.9.3
```

Installing Facter and Puppet

PuppetLabs provides the following package repositories for the latest stable version of Puppet and Facter, which automatically require the appropriate Ruby packages for their respective platforms:

- *http://apt.puppetlabs.com*: Debian, Ubuntu, DEB
- *http://yum.puppetlabs.com*: RedHat, CentOS, Fedora RPM
- *http://downloads.puppetlabs.com/mac*: MacOS DMG
- *http://downloads.puppetlabs.com/windows/*: Windows MSI

Packages provide a fast and easy way to get Puppet up and running. Since this book refers to examples from Puppet's own source code, it makes more sense to install Puppet from source. This requires cloning the source code from GitHub. The following example demonstrates how to install Puppet and Facter from GitHub into ~/*src*:

```
$ mkdir ~/src
$ cd ~/src
$ git clone https://github.com/puppetlabs/facter.git
$ git clone https://github.com/puppetlabs/puppet.git
```

Now, we need to configure the RUBYLIB environment variable to ensure that Ruby can find the Puppet and Facter source files. We also need to configure the PATH environment variable to ensure that our system can use the Facter and Puppet commands:

```
$ export RUBYLIB=~/src/facter/lib:~/src/puppet/lib:$RUBYLIB
$ export PATH=~/src/facter/bin:~/src/puppet/bin:$PATH
```

The environment variables can be either saved in a user profile file (like ~/*.bashrc*), or stored as an alias along with the Puppet/Facter commands.

Now, we can use git to check out a specific revision of Facter or Puppet:

```
$ cd ~/src/facter
$ git checkout 1.6.10
$ facter --version
1.6.10
$ cd ~/src/puppet
$ git checkout 2.7.14
$ puppet --version
2.7.14
```

If you want to use the latest version of Facter and Puppet in development, check out the *.x branch or master:

```
$ cd ~/src/facter
$ git checkout 2.x
$ cd ~/src/puppet
$ git checkout 3.0.x
```

Modules

Puppet modules are a collection of components for managing a specific service. Modules allow the greater Puppet community to share and reuse code to deploy the same service across a wide range of environments. Complex infrastructures are typically composed of several smaller modules. Examples of modules can be found at puppetlabs (*http://forge.puppetlabs.com*).

Modules conform to a directory structure that organizes content as follows:

```
module_name
  |-- manifests
  |-- files
  |-- templates
  |-- tests
  |-- lib
  `-- spec
```

Each subfolder contains the following files:

manifests
> Puppet classes and defined resource types are located in a manifest file (*.pp* extension) in this directory.

lib
> Ruby extensions (*.rb* extension) are located in this directory. This includes custom facts, functions, types, and providers.

spec
> Ruby Rspec test files are located in this directory. Rspec files are used to implement unit tests for Ruby source code or Puppet manifests.

files
> Files distributed to Puppet agents via *source* ⇒ *puppet:///modules/module_name/* are located in this directory.

templates

> Ruby ERB (**.erb*) templates are located in this directory. They are typically used by the file resource's `content` property, via *content* ⇒ *template(module_name/ some_template.erb)*.

tests

> Puppet *.pp* manifest files containing declaration of classes and resources.

Modules must conform to this directory structure so that Puppet knows how to access and use the content from modules to extend itself. All Ruby extensions for Puppet should be contained in a module's *lib* directory.

Before we can start creating any user-defined Puppet content, we must first understand how Puppet distributes custom content to puppet agents. When the Puppet package is installed on the system, only built-in native types/providers are available. Unlike manifests, files in the *lib* directory are distributed to all the Puppet agents.

> If Puppet encounters a type when applying a catalog that it cannot find, it will simply skip that type.

When running Puppet in client/server mode, custom providers need to be downloaded from the master to the agents by enabling the *pluginsync* option. When this option is enabled, the latest version of all custom types and providers will be synchronized to the agents ensuring that the latest version is always used.

> Puppet does not currently support loading multiple versions of types and providers from different environments. Types and providers should always be *pluginsync*ed from the production or default environment. Do not expect multiple versions of types and providers to work with Puppet environments (as of Puppet 3.0.0).

In order to determine the current modulepath, the following command provides a colon-separated list of directories that comprise the modulepath:

```
$ puppet config print modulepath
/etc/puppet/modules:/usr/share/puppet/modules
```

> When the puppet command is executed as a non-root user, the modulepath will include the user's home directory, which is suitable for development. When deploying the module to a Puppet server, use the root account's modulepath.

Troubleshooting and Debugging

When developing Puppet types and providers, it's not uncommon to run into bugs that are hard to trace and debug. There are a few options in Puppet that will simplify the troubleshooting process. The option `--trace` will provide the Ruby stacktrace when Puppet execution fails. This will give you a file and line number to provide additional insight into the problem at hand.

The `Puppet.debug('message')` method can be used in conjunction with the Puppet `--debug` flag to output troubleshooting messages to the console. This is helpful to output variables and ensure that certain methods are invoked as expected. But it's often far more helpful to dive directly into a debugger. The `ruby-debug` gem gives you the ability to interactively troubleshoot by breaking at a specific line in the code:

```
require 'ruby-debug'; debugger
```

The `post_mortem` option allows `ruby-debug` to enter into an interactive session when an exception occurs:

```
require 'ruby-debug';
Debugger.start(:post_mortem => true)
```

Let's update our `custom_package` resource and add a breakpoint inside the type's `exists?` method:

```
def exists?
  require 'ruby-debug'; debugger
  ...
end
```

Now when we manage a `custom_package`, the debugger drops us into an interactive session when the method `exists?` is invoked:

```
$ puppet apply -e "custom_package { 'bash': ensure=>present }"
/etc/puppetlabs/puppet/modules/custom_packages/lib/puppet/provider/custom_pack-
age/yum.rb:32
@property_hash[:ensure] == :present
(rdb:1)
```

In this interactive session we can:

- List the current source code:

```
(rdb:1) l
[27, 36] in /etc/puppetlabs/puppet/modules/custom_packages/lib/puppet/provid-
er/custom_package/yum.rb
    27      end
    28    end
    29
    30    def exists?
    31      require 'ruby-debug'; debugger
=>  32      @property_hash[:ensure] == :present
    33    end
    34
    35    def version
    36      @property_hash[:version]
```

- Print any variable values:

```
(rdb:1) p @property_hash
{:version=>"3.2-32.el5", :ensure=>:present, :name=>"bash"}
```

- Next, execute the following line of code:

```
(rdb:1) n
/opt/puppet/lib/ruby/site_ruby/1.8/puppet/property/ensure.rb:74
if result
(rdb:1)
/opt/puppet/lib/ruby/site_ruby/1.8/puppet/property/ensure.rb:75
return :present
(rdb:1)
```

- Use *irb* to enter IRB session:

```
(rdb:1) irb
irb(ensure):001:0> p Puppet[:config]
"/etc/puppetlabs/puppet/puppet.conf"
=> nil
irb(ensure):002:0> exit
```

- Continue execution of code:

```
(rdb:1) c
notice: Finished catalog run in 18.05 seconds
```

- Quit the debugger:

```
(rdb:1) q
Really quit? (y/n) y
```

This is a very shallow introduction to ruby-debug, but even with this short example the power of the debugger is clearly demonstrated. The ability to interact with the code when it's executed is tremendously useful in order to understand and troubleshoot subtle bugs. For more information on ruby-debug, see *http://bashdb.sourceforge.net/ruby-debug.html*.

About the Authors

Dan Bode has worked in the technology industry as a consultant and software developer for the past decade. He has spent most of the last four years building infrastructure automation solutions and teaching people how to use Puppet. He currently works in the Business Development at PuppetLabs, where he spends his time researching technologies and integrating them with Puppet.

Nan Liu is a Business Development Engineer at Puppet Labs and provides Puppet integration solutions for third-party partners. Prior to BD, he was part of Puppet Labs' professional service team, which travels globally to train users of Puppet and provide implementation and architectural consulting for Puppet Labs customers worldwide.

Colophon

The animal on the cover of *Puppet Types and Providers* is a hispid hare (*Caprolagus hispidus*).

The cover image is from *Shaw's Zoology*. The cover font is Adobe ITC Garamond. The text font is Adobe Minion Pro; the heading font is Adobe Myriad Condensed; and the code font is Dalton Maag's Ubuntu Mono.

Built with Atlas. O'Reilly Media, Inc., 2012.

Get even more for your money.

Join the O'Reilly Community, and register the O'Reilly books you own. It's free, and you'll get:

- $4.99 ebook upgrade offer
- 40% upgrade offer on O'Reilly print books
- Membership discounts on books and events
- Free lifetime updates to ebooks and videos
- Multiple ebook formats, DRM FREE
- Participation in the O'Reilly community
- Newsletters
- Account management
- 100% Satisfaction Guarantee

Signing up is easy:

1. **Go to: oreilly.com/go/register**
2. **Create an O'Reilly login.**
3. **Provide your address.**
4. **Register your books.**

Note: English-language books only

To order books online:
oreilly.com/store

For questions about products or an order:
orders@oreilly.com

To sign up to get topic-specific email announcements and/or news about upcoming books, conferences, special offers, and new technologies:
elists@oreilly.com

For technical questions about book content:
booktech@oreilly.com

To submit new book proposals to our editors:
proposals@oreilly.com

O'Reilly books are available in multiple DRM-free ebook formats. For more information:
oreilly.com/ebooks

Spreading the knowledge of innovators   oreilly.com

CPSIA information can be obtained
at www.ICGtesting.com
Printed in the USA
FSOW04n2034180915
11288FS